The
Ontology of
Cyberspace

The
Ontology of
Cyberspace

Philosophy, Law, and the Future of
Intellectual Property

DAVID R. KOEPSELL

OPEN COURT
Chicago and La Salle, Illinois

To order books from Open Court, call toll free 1-800-815-2280 or visit our website at www.opencourtbooks.com.

Open Court Publishing Company is a division of Carus Publishing Company.

Copyright © 2000 by Carus Publishing Company

First paperback printing 2003

Printed and bound in the United States of America.

Library of Congress Cataloging-in-Publication Data

Koepsell, David R. (David Richard)
      The ontology of cyberspace : philosophy, law, and intellectual property /
   David R. Koepsell.
         p.   cm.
      Includes bibliographical references and index.
      ISBN 0-8126-9423-6 (cloth: alk. paper) —ISBN 0-8126-9537-2 (pbk: alk. paper)
      1. Intellectual property—Methodology—Philosophy. 2. Industrial property—
   Methodology—Philosophy. 3. Copyright and electronic data processing—
   Philosophy. 4. Cyberspace—Philosophy. 5. Ontology.   I. Title.
   K1401.K64 2000
   346.04'82—dc21   00-055769

To Joanne

Brief Contents

Detailed Contents

Acknowledgments

I am indebted to Barry Smith, Mariam Thalos, and William Rapaport for their support and guidance. Many thanks must also go to Clark Hare for his helpful and provocative critiques. Thanks also to Kirsten Barclay and Patrick Lennon for their help with editing. I am grateful for my parents' support throughout. Thanks to Max Primack for setting me out on the road of philosophy.

1

Preliminary Questions

1.0 Introduction

The term "cyberspace" has recently surfaced repeatedly in the popular culture. Magazine covers and book titles use "cyberspace" and related terms to describe the vast and growing network of computers, otherwise called the Internet, which transcends national boundaries. "Cyberspace" is a term whose actual referent is, however, quite vague. Does it refer only to the network which connects computers everywhere, or does it apply to all phenomena which may occur amongst or inside computers, including interactions via networks? As the term has been used in the popular culture, it may apply to either or both. Notions about what cyberspace consists of are as vague as the designation of the term itself. It is spoken of as an "intangible" realm full of "virtual" beings. This is not surprising when the term "cyberspace" connotes a space apart from that of ordinary experience. It is with a great deal of hesitation that I use this term for, in fact, as I will argue below, cyberspace is nothing very special.

The popular culture, and unfortunately, even the few philosophical works pertaining to cyberspace, do not challenge the assumption that cyberspace is intangible, or that its objects are somehow special. In actuality, cyberspace is just another expressive medium. Since the 1960s, however, notions about the nature of media have been confused in no small part due to Marshall McLuhan whose confused and confusing mantra—"the medium is the message"—survives in almost every existing account of cyberspace. The medium is the medium and the message is the message. There is, as we will see, no theoretically sound basis to conflate the two. Moreover, everything we create purposefully is an expression in some medium.

Mistakes about these concepts have led to a confused ontology, or categorization, of cyberspace and its constituents. These mistakes have also, as a result of parallel developments, come to be reflected in a legal scheme which no longer works. What follows is an argument in support of these contentions, and a proposal for a new ontology of cyberspace and of intellectual property in general. The new ontology avoids the mistakes outlined above, and serves as a rational alternative to the myths which surround cyberspace and all computer-mediated phenomena.

1.1 Practical Considerations

Not since the first work of fiction was produced have philosophers been confronted with such an impressive and so totally unexplored new realm of ontological inquiry as is presented by cyberspace. The development of the computer and the concept of cyberspace have ushered in such a frontier. Cyberspace is something whose nature remains largely unexplored despite its ripeness for philosophical analysis.

Before attempting to approach the theoretical investigation of cyberspace from the ontological point of view, it is perhaps best to put the problems which have arisen with the concept of cyberspace in a practical context. An explanation is in order as to why cyberspace presents any problems at all and why such problems are important. The phenomenon, or range of phenomena, which have been said to comprise "cyberspace" present a number of practical problems. These problems are often made apparent through the legal issues which have arisen regarding computer-mediated phenomena.[1] All of the theoretical questions that might be posed regarding the nature of cyberspace boil down to the following questions: How shall we treat various computer-mediated phenomena in practice? Into what existing categories do such things as software, the Internet, and virtual reality fit? Each of these phenomena present specific practical problems which I will explore below.

---

1. I shall use this term interchangeably with the pop-cultural and less accurate "cyberspace."

1.11 Software

What is software? Software is the symbolic code which acts upon computers to turn certain input into specific output. Federal law defines it as a "set of statements or instructions to be used directly or indirectly in a computer to bring about a certain result."[2] Others have described software as "built from ideal infallible mathematical components, whose outputs are not affected by the components into which they feed."[3] Software consists of code, called a programming language, which when used by a computer,[4] causes the computer to do certain things. The things that the computer does depends upon how the code is organized.

Software forms the basis for all computer-mediated phenomena. A computer without software consists of nothing but switches which may be either on or off. Without some form of instruction for these switches, either etched into Read Only Memory (ROM) or loaded into Random Access Memory (RAM), the switches would sit idle.[5] But once software is introduced to these switches by way of ROMs, or loaded from such media as magnetic or optical disks or tapes into RAM, the computer can perform any number of functions.[6]

Software has confused jurists, lawyers, and those who would look to their decisions regarding the nature of software, because the law of intellectual property has typically divided the world into two discrete forms of intellectual property: (a) expressions, and (b) machines. Software looks a little like both in that it is composed of symbolic information (the programming language or machine language) which is clearly expression, and, like a

---

2. Computer Software Rental Amendments Act, 17 United States Code [hereafter, U.S.C.] Sec. 101 (1990). (I will forgo using law review citation style in all my legal citations to increase transparency in my references for non-lawyers, and for consistency. For citations to the U.S. Code and to other legal publications, the first number is the volume.)

3. The League for Programming Freedom, "Against Software Patents" in *High Noon on the Electronic Frontier,* ed. Peter Ludlow, p. 59.

4. In some cases, directly—as with a LISP machine. In other cases, the code must be "compiled" into something which the machine can read—machine language.

5. ROMs are storage devices for software consisting of binary switches which are either permanently on or permanently off. RAMs are storage devices for software consisting of switches whose on/off positions may be altered and which must remain powered to store information.

6. Early computers, such as ENIAC, consisted only of switches which, when manually switched, computed various functions. The act of flipping those switches was, in such cases, the introduction of the software to the hardware of the computer.

machine, it seems to act upon the world when introduced to computer hardware producing certain outputs. This seemingly dual nature has confounded the courts' treatment of software and confused analyses of software's true nature.

Copyright law has typically applied to written works. It protects, for a limited period of time, an author's interest in his or her original works to the extent that they are in a fixed medium of expression. Thus, the source code of a computer program, which is written in such programming languages as C, Pascal, Basic, etc., is clearly copyrightable. However, the object code, which is what source code is often compiled into so that the computer can read and act upon its instructions, has not always been so clearly copyrightable:

> It has been suggested even if the object code is analogized to a recording of a phonograph record or tape in a form that the machine can recognize and play back—such items being clearly copyrightable—the transportation of the binary code into a circuit design that replicates the on-off switching of the binary form object code using [various] . . . processes raises serious questions of copyright protectability since the work is not a "writing" *but is, in microchip form, part of a machine, a utilitarian object, and hence not copyrightable.*[7]

Machines and other such "utilitarian objects" are normally afforded the protection of patent law. "Whoever invents or discovers any new and useful process, machine, manufacture, or composition of matter, or any new and useful improvement thereof, may obtain a patent therefor. . ."[8] A patent is a limited monopoly. It grants one the right to exclude others from producing, using, or selling an invention during a specified time period.[9] Until recently, software has not been afforded patent protection. This is because it has not been clear that software is always a process, machine, manufacture, or composition of matter. Nonetheless, some limited patent protection may be available for certain software. For example, "the method which instructs a computer to perform its operating functions as distinguished

---

7. 18 American Jurisprudence (Second) [hereafter Am.Jur.2d], Copyright Sec. 51. [emphasis added]; see also Ray A. Mantle, "Trade Secret and Copyright Protection of Computer Software," *Computer Law Journal* 4 (1984), p. 669.

8. 35 U.S.C. Sec. 101 (1999); *See also* 60 Am.Jur.2d, *Patents*, Sec. 65.

from the instructions themselves, is said not to be subject to copyright but is protected, if at all, by patent law."[10] This is because the courts have determined that such methods are akin to processes, which are patentable.

Is software an idea, a written work, a process, or a machine? It has not been clear, in the law of intellectual property, what software actually is. At various times, it has been treated as each of these. It is at least clear that categorizing software is not only theoretically problematic, but that this problem results in practical difficulties as well. The legal system is working out these problems in accord with our concerns for practicality and economic efficiency, but the philosophical underpinnings of the problem remain unresolved.

1.12 The Internet

The Internet is a group of interconnected networks which has evolved more-or-less independently of any social, political, or governmental control.[11] The Internet connects computers at universities, research laboratories, businesses, government offices, and homes. Through the Internet, vast amounts of information are accessible to millions of users and e-mail and software travels instantly between continents.[12] Various entities, both governmental and private (mostly the former) have sought to enforce certain conduct on the Internet (or Net, as it has come to be called). A notable example of this has been the attempt to prevent the dissemination of strong encryption programs via the Net. The U.S. government's attempt to prevent the spread of a program called

---

9. The term of the monopoly was, until recently, for 17 years. Now, according to changes made in the law pursuant to various international trade agreements, patents grant the owner a 20-year monopoly.

10. See 18 Am.Jur. 2d, *Copyright*, Sec. 52; see, e.g., *Apple Computer, Inc. v. Franklin Computer Corp.*, 714 Federal Reporter 2d [hereafter F.2d] 1240 (3d Cir) *cert. dismissed* 104 Supreme Court Reporter [hereafter S.Ct.] 690 (1983). (Again, for the sake of non-lawyers, 714 is the volume number and 1240 is the page number of the decision. All further case cites are in this form). Since this decision, as I will show in later chapters, patent law has been extended to software extensively.

11. Although, at its roots, it evolved from military and governmental networks, it has since grown well beyond the bounds of any overarching governmental control.

12. For a discussion of the topology of the Internet as of 1994, see Michael Batty and Bob Barr, "The Electronic Frontier: Exploring and Mapping Cyberspace," *Futures*, 26 (1994), pp. 699–712.

Pretty Good Privacy (PGP) and programs like it through the Net has been justified by expression of national security concerns.[13] At the other end of the spectrum are groups such as the Electronic Frontier Foundation (EFF) which have attempted to maximize the freedom of information flow through the Net. But the question remains unanswered on either side: are programs such as PGP like the "Enigma Machine," or are they simply mathematical algorithms?[14] Determining what sort of legal entity PGP is (idea, expression, or utilitarian object) will determine what legal treatment it should be afforded. How shall the law, likewise, treat the medium of the Net? Is e-mailing a copy of PGP the same sort of act as sending an Enigma Machine through the international mails? This problem has been a source of public debate and legal dispute but has not, to date, been seriously analyzed. The Internet hosts a variety of services which pose practical and theoretical problems of categorization, including e-mail, Wide-Area Information Servers (WAIS) and hypertexts, and Usenet threads, among many others. Each of these are described briefly below.

1.12.1 E-Mail

E-Mail is somewhat like traditional post, somewhat like a telegram, and somewhat like communicating via telephone. E-mail is composed on a computer or via a computer terminal. It is like computer software in that, while it is being composed, it resides in RAM, as part of a machine, or on another storage device. E-mail, like all information on the Net, is then sent through network connections. On a telecommunications network such as the Internet, electronic information which is digitally encoded is split up into parts called "packets." These packets are all tagged with information that tells the network where the packet is from, where it is going, and how it fits back together with other packets. Thus, while e-mail is superficially like tradi-

---

13. For an explanation of PGP, See Philip R. Zimmerman, "How PGP Works/ Why Do You Need PGP," in Ludlow, p. 179; For a history of the U.S. government crackdown on strong cryptography, *See* Steven Levy, "Crypto Rebels," in Ludlow, p. 185.

14. The Enigma Machine was developed by the Germans in World War II to encrypt messages broadcast for military purposes. The possession of such machines remains severely regulated and the machine itself remains classified. On the other hand, mathematical algorithms cannot be classified, and possession of them cannot be punished.

tional mail in that it is sent and delivered as a whole, it is unlike traditional mail in that it is literally disassembled into various constituent parts and dispersed throughout a network. While in the network, the parts may take any number of different paths and be reassembled upon delivery. There are no sealed e-mail envelopes. Conversations occurring over telephone networks under new Asynchronous Transfer Mode protocols are likewise digitized and disassembled through this process of "packet-switching."

When e-mail arrives it may end up in RAM, or more typically take some place on a nonvolatile medium such as a disk drive, at which time, as copyright law would consider it, it is more like a written work or a phonograph record and less like a machine. As with software, e-mail is not clearly categorized, and seems to be like various things at various times.

1.12.2 WIDE AREA INFORMATION SERVERS

Wide Area Information Servers (WAIS) include such things as the World Wide Web (WWW), Archie Servers, and Gopher Servers.[15] Each of these services allow one to locate text, graphics, files and other forms of information on the Net. The WWW is a variation on the concept of hypertext in which, by choosing key words in documents or a multi-media "home page," a user can follow links between information. Any one WWW site may contain links to any number of other such sites. This interconnectedness of information and sites, coupled with the packet-switched networks over which all of this information flows, complicates practical and theoretical determinations of location, objecthood and, to an extent, ownership on the Net. Where is any particular web-site when it may be linked to sites anywhere on the web? Where is any information on the Net? This has been a real legal conundrum which

---

15. Users of the Internet may be familiar with the World Wide Web through using various "browsers" such as Netscape. New browsers are developed all the time. The information on the web consists of documents composed of Hyper Text Markup Language (HTML), which is a combination of the documents themselves and embedded software or commands which the browser software uses to configure the HTML documents on the "web" for viewing. These embedded programming languages are evolving all of the time as well. Currently, JAVA, from Sun Microsystems, is vying for the place of lingua franca of the web.

affects, *inter alia,* determinations of legal jurisdiction, or who may be sued or prosecuted in which courts for illegal acts on the Net.

Archie and Gopher servers pose similar problems in differing ways. Archie and Gopher are similar to WWW in that they provide links to information on the Net. However, these servers are typically used for locating and retrieving files and the means of searching Archie and "Gopherspace" are not hypertextual, but more linear. One can locate files through Archie and Gopher by entering keywords or following menus. Using WWW is more akin to wandering around cyberspace whereas using Archie and Gopher servers is more like sending or ordering out for specific information. While these analogies are not intended to import any ontological assumptions, they are useful for explaining the "feel" of using each type of service. A comprehensive ontology of cyberspace may eventually account for the feel of using different services on the Net.

1.12.3 USENET

Finally, Usenet threads represent another ontologically challenging phenomenon on the Net. Usenet is a portion of the Net devoted to the collection and distribution of articles for "newsgroups." There are thousands of newsgroups, each of which is devoted to a particular subject or discussion. Users may join newsgroups in which case all of the postings for that newsgroup are channeled to the user's e-mail account or to a news-server on the user's system. Usenet threads pose problems similar to WWW in that their location is non-specific. However, Usenet threads become distributed throughout the Net in ways unlike WWW. That is, information in a WWW site remains "at" the site and is browsed by the user remotely,[16] while Usenet threads are distributed so that there are literally thousands of copies of each posting dispersed across the entire Net.

Internet services, such as those discussed above, all pose practical and ontological problems regarding their location and objecthood due to the phenomenon of packet-switching and due to their various modes of distribution and linkage. These services

---

16. A copy of the page is reproduced in the memory of the Browser's computer.

also raise questions regarding the notions of authorship, originality, and plagiarism of works of expression. All of these problems are being made apparent through legal disputes regarding the Internet. The legal system is being forced to deal with questions whose answers are typically based upon the law's own common-sense ontology. However, the Internet and other computer-mediated phenomena are not necessarily so easily prone to categorization within that ontology.

1.13 Virtual Reality

The emerging phenomenon of virtual reality ("VR") poses a number of related problems. Virtual reality is created by software. Virtual reality is a simulated environment which may be experienced much as reality is experienced. VR is like a very detailed, immersive video game. Virtual objects may be manipulated by using some sort of interface, such as a "data-glove," which senses the position and movements of the user's hands. Other interfaces "put" the user into the virtual environment to varying degrees by sensing the movement of other limbs or the position of the user's body and by generating sensory feedback which the VR user experiences.

Clearly, virtual reality poses a number of practical problems. Suppose a virtual reality world in which users may manipulate virtual objects and "inhabit" virtual places. May such users own virtual objects? May they assert possession of virtual places to the exclusion of others? If so, by what claim of right may such ownership or possession be asserted? Would not such claims require at least a strong analogy of virtual reality to actual reality or Real Life "RL" (for want of a better distinction)?

To date, no comprehensive philosophical analysis has been made which might provide satisfactory solutions to the practical problems posed above. Rather, cyberspace is being created without any real understanding of what it is. As such, we are often at a loss for how to treat it. The Internet is a prime example of how a lack of understanding has led to conflicts. Moreover, the law provides a useful framework for discussing the theoretical problems of computer-mediated phenomena given the legal system's attempts to grapple with the conflicts which have emerged.

1.2 Theoretical Considerations

The concept of cyberspace is a vague one. Some people confuse it
with the notion of virtual reality. VR, however, is but a small
aspect of cyberspace. Even without considering the special problems posed by VR, a number of ontological questions can be
posed regarding the goings-on within and among computers. The
following questions should be explored and the implications of
their various answers likewise considered:

What is cyberspace? Is it dimensional? Are there things in
cyberspace? Are things in cyberspace properly called objects? Are
such objects, or cyberspace itself, substances or processes? Is
cyberspace or the objects in it real or ideal? What is the categorical
scheme of cyberspace? How should cyberspace fit into a broader
categorical scheme? Addressing these questions should lead to the
development of a comprehensive ontology of cyberspace.

A comprehensive ontology of cyberspace is important both
philosophically and sociologically. Philosophers desiring to understand reality typically do not exclude whole categories of phenomena from consideration. On the contrary, ontologists must strive
to account for as many phenomena as possible (at least those
which are open to ordinary experience). For this reason alone the
realm of cyberspace should be considered from an ontological
point of view. But other benefits may arise from an ontological
consideration of cyberspace. Examining computer-mediated phenomena offers a rare opportunity of a relatively constrained world
of being. Simply put, there is only as much cyberspace as we create. Such a neatly delineated realm offers the possibility for in-
depth and exhaustive study unavailable in the world of ordinary
experience over which we have a very limited control. An exhaustive ontology of cyberspace may serve as a sort of manageable laboratory for ontological exploration. Ontological methodologies
may perhaps be more easily tested in such a laboratory than in the
world at large. Finally, inquiry into the ontology of cyberspace
may shed new light on the discipline of ontology in general.

There are a number of sociological reasons for developing a
comprehensive ontology of cyberspace. Computers and computer
networks are becoming ubiquitous. As these tools permeate our
lives to ever greater degrees, so do the questions they pose and
the conflicts to which they give rise. How shall we treat cyber-

objects philosophically and practically? This question is now a very real problem. For instance, the question of whether computer software is patentable is one of real social importance. The patent scheme differs significantly from the copyright scheme and each confers starkly different benefits and burdens. The implications of our ontological decisions regarding cyberspace are too potentially far-reaching to be made without some deep reflection. Cyberspace is proliferating rapidly and how we treat it must ultimately depend upon a correct and adequate ontology which could provide a satisfactory account of the relations between computer-mediated phenomena and other types of being.

What follows is an introduction to the problem of developing a comprehensive ontology of cyberspace. A brief history of the development of cyberspace precedes the philosophical discussion. To date, the literature fails to seriously address the problem of the ontology of computer-mediated phenomena mostly because of a failure on the part of those who have attempted to do so to understand correct ontology as a discipline. Thus, I shall look first at what constitutes ontological investigation and ask how the literature which currently exists on the subject of the ontology of cyberspace fails to meet the criteria for such inquiry.

Finally, a framework for a proper (or at least careful) ontological investigation of cyberspace is proposed. This framework is one which has evolved already through the law of intellectual property and which is being applied by jurists to resolve the problems associated with software.

1.21 Cyberspace

The term "cyberspace" is a new one, coined by the science-fiction novelist William Gibson. As used in his "cyberpunk" fiction (a genre more-or-less invented by him with his novel *Neuromancer*) the term refers to what he calls a "consensual hallucination" which futuristic computer network users experience when "jacking-in" to a world-wide computer network. However, the term has come into popular usage as a name for the Internet. This term need not be confined simply to networks. If cyberspace is considered to apply to all phenomena occurring electronically "within" computers, the term's usefulness as a general descriptive term is clear. The question remains open: is cyberspace an existence or an occurrence at all or is it something quite unique? For now, the word "cyberspace" serves only as a term of entry into the topic at hand.

We may say that cyberspace developed along with computers. Any machine which takes an input and manipulates that input to form an output according to certain rules implemented through programming may be said to be a computer. Typically, we think of computers as electronic, but the first computer designed by Charles Babbage in the nineteenth century was, in fact, entirely mechanical. However, in *The Metaphysics of Virtual Reality,* Michael Heim offers the following description: "cyberspace suggests a computerized dimension where we move information about and where we find our way around data."[17] The use of the word "dimension" shows that this definition is rough and ready at best. It is imprecise and begs all of the ontological questions set forth above, although it captures a sort of general understanding of the pop-cultural notion of cyberspace.[18]

Electronic switching, first through vacuum tubes, then through transistors and silicon chips, forms the basis for all modern computerized phenomena. Computers are the medium for an increasing number of information-transactions. For the limited purpose of clarifying the term "cyberspace," these transactions shall be said to occupy, occur, or exist in cyberspace. Programming is such a transaction. Digital communication is another. The computations that computers carry out as a result of programming are such transactions. The term "cyberspace," for now, will refer to the complex of the switches and information transactions which occur by way of those switches within and among computers. E-mail exists and moves in cyberspace. Computer programs exist and function within cyberspace. Virtual

---

17. Michael Heim, *The Metaphysics of Virtual Reality,* p. 78.
18. Curiously, the term "cyberspace" is ordinarily applied only to digitally-computerized phenomena. A precursor to the modern computer, developed on paper in the nineteenth century but never completed, was Charles Babbage's entirely mechanical computer which used gears and binary mathematics. One gets the notion that, had Babbage's Difference Engine formed the basis of all modern computerization, using mechanical rather than electronic switches, there would be no cyberspace as we know it. This problem may require consideration later as we try to unravel the ontological questions pertaining to computer-mediated phenomena.

reality exists and occupies cyberspace. Financial transactions increasingly occur in cyberspace. The ontological presuppositions and problems associated with this definition and the assertions above will be discussed later.

1.22 The Ontological Problem

No serious philosophical approaches to the ontology of cyberspace have been made to date. This is not to say that it is totally undiscovered country. In fact, a few have noted that there are philosophical implications of cyberspace open for exploration:

> Cyberspace is more than a breakthrough in electronic media or in computer interface design. With its virtual environments and simulated worlds, cyberspace is a metaphysical laboratory, a tool for examining our very sense of reality.[19]

Unfortunately, the most promising title in this study, Heim's *The Metaphysics of Virtual Reality,* deals only cursorily and superficially with the ontology of cyberspace. Chapter Seven of Heim's book, entitled "The Erotic Ontology of Cyberspace," sets forth the problem quite succinctly: "We need to give an account of (1) the way entities exist within cyberspace and (2) the ontological status of cyberspace—the construct, the phenomenon—itself."[20] Heim works hastily through a number of hypotheses, including 1) that "Platonism provides the psychic makeup for cyberspace entities,"[21] and 2) that Leibniz's "logic, metaphysics, and notion of representational symbols show us the hidden underpinnings of cyberspace."[22] But Heim fails to back up these already vague hypotheses with any sound reasoning or serious discussion. Rather, we are asked to accept such statements as:

> The Central System Monad is the only being that exists with absolute necessity. Without a sysop, no one could get on line to reality. Thanks to the Central System Monad, each individual monad lives out its separate life

19. *Ibid.*, p. 83.
20. *Ibid.*, p. 84.
21. *Ibid.*, p. 81.
22. *Ibid.*, p. 92.

according to the dictates of its own willful nature while still harmonizing with all monads on line.[23]

Ultimately, Heim does not answer the ontological questions he sets forth, and only leaves us asking more questions. This lapse is forgivable considering the context of the book as a whole. Despite his qualifications as a philosopher, Heim's *The Metaphysics of Virtual Reality* is primarily a popularized account of various sociological and psychological concerns which arise with this new medium. His book focuses primarily on virtual reality instead of cyberspace as a whole. In fact, it confuses the two terms throughout. But it is a work directed at, and emerging from the popular culture surrounding cyberspace. Its concerns are not rigorously philosophical.

What then are the philosophical concerns that must be addressed in an ontological investigation of cyberspace? Answering this question requires an agreement on the role and methods of correct ontology. In practice and over time, various ontologies and their methods have differed markedly. But some philosophers have attempted to generalize about the aims of ontology as well as to formulate schemes for its accomplishment. There is at least a general consensus among philosophers that ontology is the study of, variously: existence, being, reality and/or the meaning of each of these words.[24] Thus, an ontology of cyberspace would consider these matters as applied to the phenomena which we agree to constitute or comprise cyberspace. Although Heim fails to adequately address these concerns, the problem is clear given an understanding of the general subject of ontology.[25]

1.23   *The Legal Framework for the Ontology of Cyberspace*

To date, the ontology of the law has not been adequately analyzed. Adolf Reinach's "The A Priori Theory of Right", published

---

23. *Ibid.*, p. 99.
24. See, for instance, C.J.F. Williams, *What Is Existence?*, p. 1; Ingvar Johansson, *Ontological Investigations*, p. 1; Nicolai Hartmann, *New Ways of Ontology*, p. 11.
25. Mark D. Pesce makes some interesting observations about the psychological phenomena regarding cyberspace, or more accurately, how people experience computer-mediated phenomena and the various psychological phenomena associated with that experience.

in 1913, is an excellent foray into this wide-open field of inquiry, but little has been done in this area since. The ontological status of legal objects and entities has been largely ignored in the branch of philosophy typically referred to as the Philosophy of Law. Adolf Reinach noted the existence of *a priori* legal objects, and others have noted the existence of cultural objects, such as practices.[26] The legal system consists of both *a priori* and cultural objects. The objects of the law, embodied in legal codes and the common law, have been created or recognized by legislators and jurists without regard to the tools employed in correct ontology, and the naive ontology embodied in the law is in need of rigorous critical analysis. Recently, progress in the emerging area of applied metaphysics has been made, specifically in the area of the ontology of geography and real estate.[27] The ontology of law should be similarly addressed. Most notably, John Searle has added to the literature investigating generally the nature of social objects.[28]

While philosophers have not yet adequately addressed the ontological problems presented by cyberspace, the legal system has been grappling with the practical problems raised by the emergence of computerized media. Intellectual property law has developed a useful categorical scheme which may be readily used as a point of departure for an ontological study of cyberspace. The usefulness of this categorical scheme is partly due to the fact that the law of intellectual property has been built around a crude ontology. What follows is the legal categorical scheme for intellectual property, ranging from those objects which are afforded the least legal protection to those which are afforded the most.

See Mark D Pesce, "The Final Amputation: Pathogenic Ontology in Cyberspace," presented at the Third International Conference on Cyberspace (1993).

26. *See, e.g., Practical Knowledge: Outlines of a Theory of Traditions and Skills,* ed. J.C. Nyiri, and Barry Smith (New York: Croom Helm, 1988), 172-209. A priori objects exist by virtue of natural relationships amongst objects as opposed, for instance, to objects which exist by fiat.

27. Barry Smith, "On Drawing Lines on a Map" in *Spatial Information Theory: A Theoretical Basis for GIS,* ed. Andrew U. Frank and Werner Kuhn, (Lecture Notes in Computer Science 988), (Berlin/Heidelberg/New York, 1995); Roberto Casati and Achille Varzi, *Holes and Other Superficialities* (Cambridge, Massachusetts: MIT Press, 1994); Barry Smith and Leonardo Zaibert, "Law, Ecology, Land and Credit: An Investigation in the Comparative Ontology of Real Estate and Landed Property" Research Proposal 1996. http://wings.buffalo.edu/philosophy/faculty/smith/articles/lz.html.

28. John Searle, *The Construction of Social Reality* (New York: Free Press, 1995).

1.23.1 OBJECTS WHICH ARE NOT COPYRIGHTABLE OR PATENTABLE

Ideas, procedures, natural processes, systems, concepts, laws of nature, principles, information and utilitarian works (such as recipes or instructions) are all generally outside the scope of legal protection.

1.23.2 OBJECTS WHICH ARE COPYRIGHTABLE

Expressions, both their "literal" and "nonliteral" elements, are protected by copyright to various degrees. The fundamental essence or structure of an expressive object, such as a novel's unique settings, characters, plot, etc., are all considered to be the expression's nonliteral elements and may be the subject of copyright protection, with certain exceptions.[29]

The literal elements of an expressive work are the expressions of original ideas, as distinguished from the ideas themselves, when reduced to a tangible medium of expression from which they can be perceived, reproduced, or otherwise communicated either directly or with the aid of a machine or device. The words on this page, strung together as they are, are this work's literal elements.

1.23.3 NON-EXPRESSIVE OBJECTS WHICH HAVE LIMITED PROTECTION

Certain formulas, patterns, devices or compilations of information used in a business which give a competitive advantage over competitors are afforded trade secret protection. Trade secrets are not protected against independent discovery. A trade secret need not achieve the level of advancement needed for patent protection.

1.23.4 OBJECTS WHICH ARE PATENTABLE

Utilitarian objects,[30] machines, certain processes, manufactures or compositions of matter typically also called "inventions" are all

---

29. A parody may use the non-literal elements of the work it parodies without violating copyrights.

30. Tools and implements are called "tangible" utilitarian *objects*, as opposed to utilitarian *works* mentioned above (recipes, instructions, and so forth).

afforded patent protection which gives the patent holder the exclusive right to the art disclosed. Copyright protects only the expression of an idea. Patents protect the means of reducing an inventive idea to practice.

1.24 *The Naive Ontology in the Law of Intellectual Property*

The categorical scheme above seems to reflect a certain ontology or at least a recognition of a distinction between types and tokens. Thus, this scheme will suffice as a foundation for a foray into the ontological investigation of cyberspace. It is a ready-made bridge constructed by the legal system between the practical and theoretical problems posed by computer-mediated phenomena.

As noted above, the courts have begun the theoretical task by trying to fit software into this scheme. The problems and reasoning applicable to software are also applicable by extension to the phenomena associated with the Internet and virtual reality. The questions set forth at the beginning of 1.2 above may all be addressed within the categorical scheme developed in the law of intellectual property.

1.3 The Task Ahead

What has been presented above is an attempt to outline the problems posed by the concept of cyberspace and a methodology for commencing an inquiry into the ontology of computer-mediated phenomena. Such an ontology should provide answers for the questions presented in section 1.2 above. By following the reasoning used by the courts and already applied to intellectual property disputes regarding software, and by analyzing the existing ontology of intellectual property and its possible flaws, a useful and comprehensive ontological approach to cyberspace may be developed.[31]

---

31. Lawrence Lessig's *Code and Other Laws of Cyberspace* (New York: Basic Books, 1999) excellently summarizes the current state of Internet law. However, his calls for more legislation and increased regulation of this medium are not backed by a sound ontology which would distinguish this medium from any other.

2

Ontology: Its Correct Object and Method

Before beginning an ontological analysis of cyberspace, it is a good idea to define clearly the goals and methods of ontology. In so doing, I will address errors which have been made by others in considering the ontology of cyberspace. These errors are useful starting points both for the larger purpose of this work and for a general introduction to ontology.

The investigation of the nature of the world, or reality, has been an overarching project of philosophy since its inception. Debates about the nature of reality have been as long-lived as the study of philosophy. The study of ontology, which is that part of philosophy concerned with the nature of being, and of metaphysics, the broad branch of philosophy to which ontology belongs, are marked by at least two distinct and seemingly irreconcilable schools of thought. The dispute between idealists and realists marks the greatest divergence in schools of thought devoted to the study of metaphysics. Very simply put, idealists order the universe in such a way that the mind, or ideas, are fundamental, whereas naturalists and realists hold that the physical universe is fundamental, and that minds and ideas are reducible to or dependent for their existence upon real (usually material) things. These two schools of metaphysics seem irreconcilable. If there are such divergent schools of thought in metaphysics, then how can a correct ontology of cyberspace be developed? First, there is a distinction between metaphysics and ontology.[1]

---

1. This section will not be an attempt to set forth or contrast *all* forms of realism and idealism, for there are many differing types of each. Rather, I will contrast the two in their most basic forms.

2.1 Metaphysics

The term "metaphysics" owes its origins to Aristotle's disciples' classification of certain miscellaneous chapters of their master's lectures as "The Metaphysics." These chapters may have been so labeled for no greater reason than that they followed the chapter on the Physics.[2] Aristotle's *Metaphysics* deals with the nature of all being, but his treatment is centered around the category of substance:

> It is clear then that it is the work of one science also to study the things that are, *qua* being. But everywhere science deals chiefly with that which is primary, and on which the other things depend, and in virtue of which they get their names. If, then, this is substance, it will be of substances that the philosopher must grasp the principles and the causes.[3]

Substance, for Aristotle, means primarily living things such as man and animals, objects which are independent or, in other words, such as to exist on their own without requiring the support of other entities. In Aristotle's metaphysics, universals exist in the substances which instantiate them. This viewpoint is in contrast with that of Plato who holds that there is a realm of being separate and apart from that of particulars.

2.11 Plato's Metaphysics

Plato conceived of all objects as existing in two separate modes. In the world of experience are particulars, such as the particular chair you are sitting in or the table at which you eat your dinner. There is also the realm of eternal, unchanging Ideals or Forms which is, for Plato, more real than the world of experience. The Forms include all properties of experience which may be called universals. Thus, whiteness is a form, roundness is a form, virtue is also a form. In his dialogue, *The Meno,* Plato elucidates the concept of the Forms with the example of the uneducated slave-boy's knowledge of geometry. According to Plato, knowledge is simply

2. Ando Takatura, *Metaphysics: A Critical Survey of Its Meaning,* p. 7.
3. Aristotle, *Metaphysics,* Book IV, Ch. 2.

recollection of the Forms with which each soul has become familiar before its current life. After walking the slave-boy through a
geometric proof, which he could not have been taught, Socrates
(Plato's mouthpiece in his Dialogues) explains to Meno,
Socrates's partner:

> Do you see, Meno, what advances [the slave-boy] has made in his power of
> recollection? He did not know at first, and he does not know now, what is
> the side of a figure of eight feet: but then he thought that he knew, and
> answered confidently as if he knew, and had no difficulty, and neither knows
> nor fancies that he knows.[4]

Later, Socrates explains the source of the slave-boy's knowledge:

> And if there have been always true thoughts in him, both at the time when
> he was and was not a man, which only need to be awakened into knowledge
> by putting questions to him, his soul must have always possessed this knowl-
> edge, for he always either was or was not a man.[5]

For Plato, the realm of the Ideals is primary, and the world of
experience of particulars is secondary. Plato's famous allegory of
the cave regards the world of particulars in which we all live as
analogous to a cave and all we see is shadows on the wall reflect-
ing the world outside. The world outside the cave is the realm of
the Ideals or Forms.

2.12 Aristotle's Metaphysics

In contrast to Plato's doctrine of the Forms is Aristotle's imma-
nentistic realism.[6] Aristotle's metaphysics rests on an empirical
approach. That is, he looks to the world of experience for answers
about the nature of reality. The bulk of Aristotle's work consists
of empirical studies of the world around him. Aristotle's approach
betrays his trust in the world of experience while Plato's results

---

4. Plato, *Meno*, Part I, p. 32.
5. *Ibid.*, p. 35.
6. Roman Ingarden, *Time and Modes of Being*, p. 3–4.

from a distrust of sense-perception. Aristotle's *ontology* is correctly termed realist. Modern realist metaphysicians include G.E. Moore and William James, among many others. The primary distinction between idealists and realists is the latter's rejection of a realm of being beyond that which is perceived. Both Plato and Aristotle are realists about universals, but Plato sees universals as existing in a transcendent realm (a sort of heaven) while Aristotle sees them as immanent to the substances in this world.

   With competing schools of metaphysics so starkly contrasting with one another, how can any method of ontology be termed "correct"? Only by understanding the difference between metaphysics and ontology may correct ontology be pursued. What is clear is that Michael Heim's *Metaphysics of Virtual Reality* contains an incorrect ontology and a muddled metaphysics.

2.2 The Incorrect Ontology of Cyberspace

In his chapter entitled "The Erotic Ontology of Cyberspace," Michael Heim makes much of the parallels which he claims exist between the Platonic Ideals and cyberspace. He writes, for instance:

> Cyberspace is Platonism as a working product. The cybernaut seated before us, strapped into sensory-input devices, appears to be, and is indeed, lost to this world. Suspended in computer space, the cybernaut leaves the prison of the body and emerges in a world of digital sensation.[7]

This paragraph is more metaphor than metaphysics. First of all, the second sentence is obviously untrue if taken literally. Computer users do not become "indeed, lost to this world" in any literal sense. Secondly, this selection refers only to one particular aspect of cyberspace: virtual reality. But before discussing the ontological error of attributing ideal being to cyberspace, I will allow Heim to try to explain this passage:

---

7. Heim, p. 89.

This Platonism is thoroughly modern, however. Instead of emerging in a sensationless world of pure concepts, the cybernaut moves among entities that are well formed in a special sense. The spatial objects of cyberspace proceed from the constructs of Platonic imagination not in the same sense that perfect solids or ideal numbers are Platonic constructs, but in the sense that inFORMation [sic] in cyberspace inherits the beauty of Platonic FORMS [sic]. The computer recycles ancient Platonism by injecting the ideal content of cognition with empirical specifics.[8]

Heim has himself rejected Platonism with the above-quoted passage. If objects in cyberspace are, in fact, spatial as he claims, then they cannot be Platonic Ideals. This implicit admission becomes even more apparent through his attribution of cyberspatial entities with "empirical specifics." Heim makes no case for Platonism as anything more than a metaphor for cyberspace.

Heim's mistake is confusing epistemology with metaphysics as well as a total disregard for the distinction between ontology and metaphysics. Recall that Heim noted the absence of an ontology of cyberspace earlier and called for developing such an ontology.[9] The irreconcilable schism between idealists and realists is a problem of epistemology, that is, that branch of philosophy which is concerned with the nature and sources of knowledge. This schism need not prevent idealists and realists from agreeing upon an *ontological* approach. Heim has subscribed to a Platonic metaphysics, at least superficially, but failed to show that cyberspatial objects were anything more than metaphorically related to Platonic ideals. What he has failed to do is to develop an ontology of cyberspace, that is, to show how cyberspatial objects fit into a categorization of other experiential objects.

2.3 Ontology vs. Epistemology and Metaphysics

Epistemology is the study of knowledge, or more specifically of how we may come to know things. Platonism posits the existence of universals with which we become familiar when our souls

---

8. *Ibid.*
9. *See* Section 1.22, *supra*.

encounter them at times prior to our current lives. For Platonists, the world of experience is but a pale reflection of the eternal realm of unchanging forms. We cannot, according to this metaphysics, know particulars with certainty and our knowledge of particulars is not as worthwhile as our recollection of the universals, which are eternal, unchanging, ideal and true.

This metaphysical viewpoint is criticized by modern realists and naturalists: "[S]uch an appeal to a realm of entities over and above concrete objects in space and time is empty verbalism, devoid of explanatory value."[10] Similarly, A.J. Ayer noted that "[n]o statement which refers to a 'reality' transcending the limits of all possible sense-experience can possibly have any literal significance."[11] These criticisms are leveled at the limitations which Platonistic metaphysics imposes upon the development of an ontology. Rejecting the world of sense-experience as little more than shadows of a greater reality makes inquiry into the world of experience seem pointless. However, an ontology need not be concerned with whether the world of experience is in fact the truest world. Rather, ontology can proceed despite differences regarding the nature of reality. This is how ontology is different from metaphysics.

As W.V. Quine stated:

the abstract entities which are the substance of mathematics—ultimately classes and classes of classes and so on up—are . . . [e]pistemologically . . . myths on the same footing with physical objects and gods, neither better nor worse except for differences in the degree to which they expedite our dealings with sense experiences.[12]

This sums up the manner in which a commonsense ontology can be developed without regard to the questions of metaphysics—namely, those questions which inquire into the ultimate reality of the objects of inquiry. An acceptance of the use of common terms which refer to objects commonly understood, and the relations which may exist between those terms and our experi-

10. W.V Quine, "On Universals," *Journal of Symbolic Logic* 12(3) (1947), pp. 74–84.
11. A.J. Ayer, "The Elimination of Metaphysics," *Language, Truth, and Logic.*
12. W.V. Quine, "Two Dogmas of Empiricism," p. 42.

ences, is all we need in order to categorize the world. Developing a commonsense ontology requires an admission that we cannot satisfactorily answer the ultimate metaphysical questions regarding what may be real and what may not be real. Rather, it requires only an acceptance of the facts of common experience, without regard to their deeper reality.

2.4 Toward a Commonsense Ontology (Toward Metaphysical Neutrality)

A realist may believe that the primary substance of the universe is physical and that everything which exists, including minds and ideas, derives from and depends upon the physical world. Would such a belief preclude the realist from agreeing with an idealist that a certain type of object relates in such and such a way to another type of object? If it would, then the ontological task of categorizing experience is faced with considerable difficulties. However if such agreements can be made, then ontology can be pursued without regard to broader metaphysical differences.[13]

Assume that there stand before us, or may appear to stand before us, two objects, A and B. I am a realist and you are an idealist. Despite our metaphysical differences, we may, through observation and experiment, come to terms regarding various apparent attributes of A and B. That is, we may agree that A has (or appears to both of us to have) a certain extension, dimension, color, weight, flavor, smell, heft, and so forth. A and B may have certain attributes in common, or certain differences upon which we may agree. A may be smaller than B, more shiny than B, heavier than B, and so on. We may agree as to our perceptions of these attributes despite our differences regarding the question of *how* A and B have those attributes.

Even an idealist will likely avoid A if I tell him that it exhibits a dangerous amount of radioactive decay. The idealist who will not heed such a warning by shrugging it off and explaining that the danger of A's radioactive decay is but a product of our minds will

---

13. *See* Barry Smith, "On Substances, Accidents, and Universals: In Defence of a Constituent Ontology."

be a dead idealist. Even idealists do not discount the apparent attributes of objects as "only" the products of consciousness; rather they admit that these attributes, whether or not they are separate and apart from consciousness, nonetheless affect or seem to affect different persons similarly.

Moreover, although I may disagree with you regarding the manner in which object A has certain attributes, after we agree as to what A's attributes are, we may compare A with B.[14] Having before us two objects we may successfully decide that they relate to each other in certain ways. These comparisons are independent of our metaphysical disagreements as to the ultimate reality of A and B. This is a conception similar to that of A.J. Ayer, who holds that Quine goes too far by speaking of ontological commitments implicit in linguistic frameworks. Ayer believes that Rudolf Carnap does not go far enough in that Carnap holds that all that can be done is an analysis of linguistic frameworks. Rather, Ayer believes that we may find it "convenient to speak of things using a given framework and yet not want to become ontologically committed to the objects of that language."[15]

None of the metaphysical differences we may have need preclude agreement as to the categorizing or ordering of the objects referred to in our ordinary language. We may come to agreements regarding relations between perceived things without agreement as to the nature or reality of the things themselves. The method and the tools we employ will be observation and language, although we may disagree as to the relative importance of both in ordering the universe. By analysis of commonly used terms, and of things apparently perceived in common experience, we may each, through the careful use of language and observation, agree upon the apparent order of the universe, at least insofar as we experience it.

A commonsense ontology should thus account for phenomena in a metaphysically neutral manner—that is, without regard to

---

14. Barry Smith, in "Formal Ontology, Common Sense, and Cognitive Science," *International Journal of Human-Computer Studies*, 43 (1995), pp. 641–667, describes the process of "commonsense realism" which I employ in the rest of this paper. *Ibid.*, p. 644. This method stands in stark contrast to "linguistic idealism" which posits that "the world exists (or has the structure which it has) in virtue of the language we use to speak about it." *Ibid.*

15. A.J. Ayer, *Metaphysics and Common Sense*, p. 52.

whether or not the objects of our common perceptions are real in some ultimate sense. Of course, the objects of our perception may include any object of thought. Objects in a commonsense ontology cannot be limited to everyday physical objects; they must include any object of thought and speech, including happiness, Bosnia, and the color white. A commonsense ontology which excludes anything given in our common experience as a possible object would be metaphysically biased.

2.41 Commonsense Ontology in the Non-Philosophical Realm

The notion of a commonsense ontology is not unique to a specialist ontology of cyberspace such as is presented here, nor is it exclusive to twentieth-century philosophy in general. We all utilize a naive ontology every day. The language we use is loaded with terms which denote an ordering of objects of experience. Much of our day-to-day conversation centers around the classification of things. Debates in every social, scientific, political, and academic arena frequently concern minor differences between objects of those various studies. These debates are not ontological in the strictest sense, but they are at the root of commonsense ontology.

Ontology as we conceive it is distinct from what has typically been called metaphysics. Metaphysics is the study of being *qua* being. But such a study, because of the irreconcilable differences in metaphysical viewpoints discussed above, faces considerable obstacles. As a matter of ideology, there will always be those who stubbornly believe that there is a realm of being separate and apart from that of experience. There will also always be those who just as stubbornly maintain that there is only one realm of being. As between these two camps, the question cannot be resolved in any easy way. Yet this question is at the very foundation of metaphysics.

Ontology, on the other hand, is simply the study of being. It can be pursued in spite of all the unresolvables of metaphysics. All of the natural sciences are models for ontology. Each inquires into the world and its structure without bothering with seemingly unsolvable questions of the sort raised by metaphysicians.

Ontology involves more than simply resolving the terms we use to classify objects. The authors of dictionaries are not practicing ontology. Rather, ontology must be something more than looking for a consensus regarding the usages of words. In categorizing the objects of the universe, ontologists must keep an eye on certain values such as logical consistency and practical applicability. Correct ontology must also at least a) correspond to every ordinary person's perception of objects and b) serve as a guide for the perception of new objects.

We categorize objects for many purposes. Categories are important social and political tools. For instance, we distinguish between so-called tangible objects and wavelengths of radiation for numerous reasons. We can hold tangible objects. We can clearly own tangible objects. We can reproduce tangible objects so that one such object and another may be exact duplicates of one another so that I may hold, own, transfer, or break one while you may do what you will with another. In these ways, tangible objects differ from wavelengths of radiation. Whether or not a tangible object such as A, or a wavelength of radiation such as X, are actually real in a metaphysical sense, we may observe certain qualities of each which are shared. For instance, A and X may each be experienced. A wavelength of radiation can be perceived through a receiver for that wavelength (for instance, a radio receiver). Object A may be held in one's hand. The differences between A and X, however, are clearly important. Thus, the law treats radio broadcasts in the form of wavelengths of radiation very differently than it does "tangible" objects of the sort one might hold in one's hand.

A radio broadcast, X, for example, will exist forever after, because the radio waves of which it is composed will propagate in space forever after. Tangible object A may likewise last forever. Both may be experienced by perception. But each of these objects is dramatically different from the other. We use the term "tangible object" to refer to rather slow-moving, relatively cohesive complexes of matter. Tangible objects take up a limited amount of space and do not change dramatically over time. Tangible objects are easily prone to a certain type of ownership, possession, or control to the exclusion of others. We are beings which tend to place a high importance upon ownership, possession, and control. Radio broadcasts, however, are not so easily prone to ownership, possession, or control. Because they propagate so rapidly and are so easily intercepted by others who have the right amplification mechanisms, the differences discussed above become exceedingly important. Despite certain fundamental similarities between A and X, we do not speak of radio waves as tangible objects. I cannot own X the way I may own A.

Much of our language concerns the classification of objects. Such classification typically revolves around the relative importance of objects to us. The importance of objects often depends upon the roles such objects play in our lives and upon the importance we place upon certain acts or states of affairs. It is because we value possession, ownership, and control that the differences between a tangible object and a wavelength of radiation are so prominent and warrant classification of each as distinct types of objects. This is but one example of the ways in which our language comes to embody an ontology based upon commonsense distinctions amongst objects.

2.42 The Commonsense Ontology of the Law

The U.S. legal system involves classifications of objects. In fact, property (tangible goods) is (approximately) nine-tenths of the law. Anglo-American law recognizes three general types of property: chattels (ordinary or tangible goods), real property (land), and intellectual property. These three categories might further be broken down into numerous subcategories. For instance, the law treats cash differently than jewels because cash has been decided to be an object whose value is as a medium of exchange, while jewels are considered to have value for other reasons and purposes.

This general categorical scheme is founded upon or comprises a certain ontology. That ontology recognizes that certain objects are more prone to certain types of acts or states of affairs than other sorts of objects. Ontology may be useful for discovering the bases for categorizations such as those embodied by or undertaken in the law. It may likewise be useful, once the bases for categorization are understood, as a means of criticism of general categorical schemes. Finally, through ontology, categorical schemes may be perfected so that they can accommodate the introduction of new objects.

The law embodies a naive ontology in its categorization of different types of legal objects. Beyond the law of property, one might consider such things as rights and duties from an ontological point of view. My point is not that the law prefers a certain type of object to another (for example, property to right). Certain rights are said to be "inalienable," and thus more important than other types of objects. Thus, it is not the fact that certain types of legal objects are "tangible" while others are not that makes objects important in a legal ontology. Legal rights are certainly not tangible. Rather, the law recognizes that certain objects are more prone to certain important acts or states of affairs. The fact of this recognition by the law can of course be examined, agreed upon, and criticized without concerning oneself with the metaphysical question about whether rights are real or not.

A commonsense ontology of the law may in general proceed as in the example above. The law of rights, for instance, could be explored fully. Rather than beginning with a general inquiry into rights, one could limit one's study specifically to legal opinions or treatises provided by judges or lawyers regarding rights. The point of such an inquiry would not be to discover the philosophical bases for rights. That question is debated by philosophers, not by those who practice jurisprudence. Rather, the point of looking at the common law, embodied in legal decisions, would be to discover how, in determining practical questions, judges and legislators have come to categorize rights within the general scheme of the law and, even more generally, in the world as a whole. Such an ontological inquiry should reveal some basis for the legal category of rights, how rights fit into a broader legal ontology, and the pre-eminence of certain rights over others. Through this process, one might be able to develop an understanding of the practical bases for the legal ontology and then investigate whether the legal ontology is internally consistent and adequate to meet various practical concerns.

An understanding of the practical bases for our categorization of objects is crucial. Once the practical bases for the categorization of rights, for instance, is understood, an ontologist of the law may proceed to examine whether the categorization of rights embodied by the law is consistent with a broader categorization of legal objects and, ultimately, objects in general. Having examined the legal ontology as it exists, and the practical concerns which the law seeks to address, a legal ontologist may then criticize the legal ontology of rights for inconsistencies or inadequacies. Or, he may decide that the inconsistencies are the result of a faulty ontology of things in general, whereas the legal ontology of rights may be perfectly fine.

2.5 The Project So Far

The method outlined above, and which will be employed, is a) a dissection of the legal ontology of intellectual property, b) an examination of that ontology's application to computer-mediated phenomena, c) a criticism of the existing ontology of cyberspace discovered in a and b, and finally, d) a re-evaluation of the ontology of intellectual property and proposal for a new categorization of its objects.

The law of intellectual property has developed a naive ontology.[16] That ontology is built around distinctions which have been drawn in the law between expressions and utilitarian objects. Expressions and utilitarian objects, moreover, have been distinguished from other types of legal objects. The naive ontology of the law of intellectual property will be studied and criticized using the tools of, and from the point of view of, commonsense realism.[17]

Commonsense realists hold that there are true and false commonsense beliefs. A theory of the commonsense world must embrace only those commonsense beliefs which are true. For instance, certain objects exist *a priori* and others exist according to certain cultural determinants. A theory of the commonsense world cannot deny the existence of *a priori* objects, but may recognize the existence of other, culturally generated objects. The next chapter will further elaborate the ontological method I will employ. Because the law of intellectual property embodies a crude ontology of cyberspace, I will approach the problem of developing a commonsense ontology of cyberspace through the methods of legal ontology. Those methods are set forth below.

---

16. As opposed to a commonsense ontology, naive ontologies are developed without regard to the rules of logic or common sense.
17. *See* Smith 1995.

3

Some Methodologies of Legal Ontology

3.1 Principles

Ontology is the study of being. Ontology is distinct from metaphysics which is typically considered to be the study of being qua being. All of the natural sciences employ the tools of ontology in the categorization of natural objects, classes, and laws. A legal ontology is a categorization of legal objects as applied by, or embodied in legal systems. Applied legal ontology is that branch of philosophy which is dedicated to the study, criticism, and evaluation of existing and possible legal ontologies. This study is founded at least upon the following principles:

I   Legal systems comprise, in part, categorizations of entities which, when created without reference to formal ontology, may or may not be "crude" or "naive" ontologies,[1] but which are nonetheless ontologies.

II   A "correct" ontology conforms exactly with logical laws.

III   Existing legal systems may or may not comprise correct ontologies.

IV   When existing legal ontologies do not comprise correct ontologies, certain practical problems, inefficiencies, or injustices may arise as a consequence.

---

1. A crude or naive ontology is one which is not necessarily a correct ontology. In other words, its categories may violate the laws of noncontradiction or excluded middle, or other logical laws.

V   When legal systems consist of correct ontologies, the
    problems which may be associated with incorrect ontolo-
    gies may be better avoided.

The applied legal ontologist has a hefty burden[2] given these
principles. The study of legal ontologies is, for the applied legal
ontologist, more than an intellectual pursuit, rather, it carries with
it the impetus of social change. Moreover, the objects of his study
are infinite, as all of the objects in the world, past and present,
sensible and intelligible, are encompassed by this study. A further
complication to the task of applied legal ontology is the choice of
a proper and manageable method for the study of any particular
legal object. The following are two choices of method available
for the applied legal ontologist.

A Note about Methodology:

These are by no means the only choices for this study. Moreover,
the practice of legal ontology is, I maintain, an exercise in commonsense ontology as described in Chapter 2. It is not dependant
upon the methodology I employ, nor are my ultimate conclusions
about the nature of cyberspace dependant upon this methodology.
My conclusions and argument are, at all times, based upon commonsense distinctions amongst objects, some of which are legal
objects. I think it is important to examine the historical
antecedents to this study, and due regard for the history and
importance of the study of legal ontology compels me to discuss
them here.

3.2   The Approach from First Principles

One perfectly plausible approach to applied legal ontology
(though not the only approach) is to examine and develop categories of legal objects without reference to existing legal categories, but rather to do so from first principles. An example of
this approach is Adolf Reinach's examination of the ontology of
claims in *The A Priori Foundations of the Civil Law*.[2] In this trea-

---

2. John F. Crosby, trans. in *Aletheia*, III (1983).

tise, first published in 1913, Reinach develops a rich and convincing ontology of the rights, obligations, social, and psychological facts associated with the legal object which we call a claim.

Reinach's methodology can best be described as an approach from first principles. That is, he examines such complex social phenomena as claims (or contracts) by looking at each and every element, both psychological and social, which comprises as a matter of necessity the social object called a claim.³ These first principles are not arrived at by any complex anthropological research. Nor does Reinach examine the existing laws of contract around the world or within various cultures. Rather, his is a method of introspection which has been engaged in by other philosophers of the social sciences in the continental tradition. Franz Brentano utilized the same method of study in his *Psychology from an Empirical Standpoint* (1874). Brentano's empiricism is based upon the view that we can discover general laws, the object of all science, by uncovering necessary relations in ordinary experience.⁴ This method may also be called "methodological essentialism,"⁵ or "methodological individualism."⁶

Methodological individualism, employed by Reinach in his examination of claims, is described best in Carl Menger's *Investigations into the Method of the Social Sciences with Special Reference to Economics.*⁷ Menger attempted to determine the "exact laws" of economics and, in so doing, assailed the "realistic-empirical" method of classical economics which:

> offers us in all realms of the world of phenomena results which are formally imperfect, however important and valuable they may be for human knowledge and practical life. They are theories which give us only a deficient understanding of the phenomena, only an uncertain prediction of them, and by no means an assured control of them.⁸

---

3. *See* John Searle, *The Construction of Social Reality* (New York: Free Press, 1995). Searle describes social objects in a very modern and thorough way, but Carl Menger, Reinach, and other early Austrians did very significant work on social objects.
4. Barry Smith, *Austrian Philosophy* (Chicago: Open Court, 1994), p. 32.
5. *See* Karl Popper, *The Poverty of Historicism*, 2d ed. (New York: Harper and Row, 1964), p. 28.
6. Smith (1994), p. 17.
7. Ed. Louis Schneider, trans. Francis J. Nock (New York: New York University Press, 1985).
8. *Ibid.*, p. 59.

According to Menger, there are two types of knowledge: a) individual, and b) general. Only general knowledge affords one an understanding of phenomena:

> Either there are concrete phenomena in their position in space and time and their concrete relationships to one another, or else there are the empirical forms recurring in the variation of these, the knowledge of which forms the object of our scientific interest. The one orientation of research is aimed at cognition of the concrete, or more correctly, of the individual aspect of phenomena; the other is aimed at cognition of their general aspect.[9]

Menger criticizes the realistic-empirical method of the sciences as poorly suited to determining exact laws of human phenomena:

> real human phenomena are not strictly typical [and] just for this reason, and also as a result of the freedom of the human will . . . empirical laws of absolute strictness are out of the question in the realm of human activity.[10]

According to Menger, exact laws of human phenomena cannot be derived from standard empirical social research. But it is those exact laws which must be the object of the study of human phenomena:

> [Exact theory is] an aim which research pursues in the same way in all realms of the world of phenomena, [it] is the determination of the strict laws of phenomena which do now present themselves as absolute, but which in respect to the approaches to cognition by which we attain to them simply bear within themselves the guarantee of absoluteness.[11]

How can exact laws of human phenomena be investigated if standard empirical study must fail? The key to the correct methodology lies in recognizing the correct "object-world" of one's study. In the case of almost all human phenomena, it is human consciousness whose role is central.[12] Exact laws of social

9. *Ibid.*, p. 35.

10. Carl Menger, *Problems of Economics and Sociology,* trans. Francis J. Nock, ed. Louis Schneider (Urbana: University of Illinois Press, 1963), p. 214.

11. Menger, *Investigations,* p. 59.

12. *See* Barry Smith, "Austrian Economics and Austrian Philosophy," in *Austrian Economics,* ed. Wolfgang Grassl and Barry Smith (London: Croom Helm, 1986), p. 1.

phenomena can be formulated or discovered only by uncovering the laws of thought which comprise those phenomena. Menger concludes that:

> The error of the social philosophers consists in the fact that they try to arrive at exact social laws by means of empirical research, and thus in a way in which exact laws of phenomena cannot be established at all, neither exact social laws nor exact natural laws.[13]

Yet the method employed by Menger in the study of economics, and by Reinach in the study of claims, is a form of empirical study. It is distinct from typical empirical research in that the subject of this study may well be one's own mental acts or states and the method employed is that of introspection. According to Menger, introspection is actually the "only logically admissible epistemology for the economist *qua* researcher."[14] Only through introspection may the researcher of social phenomena discover the exact laws which underlie those phenomena.[15]

It seems that Searle's recent discussion of social objects implicitly recognizes Menger's conclusions, though Searle does not give us an in-depth analysis of his methodology. Rather, his discussion of the nature of social objects (as, for instance, x's which count as y's in contexts c's), does not distinguish between the inner and the public phenomena which create social objects. This is a commonsense approach which I favor. I think that due regard must be paid to the origins of the study of social objects.

Reinach's analysis of the nature of claims does not rely upon any historical or legal analysis of contracts. Rather, Reinach uses Menger's method of introspection to discover the simplest constitutive elements of claims *per se*. He asks only what acts or states of affairs are necessary and sufficient conditions for the existence of claims in the world. Reinach concludes that claims arise when people make promises which are accompanied by both an inward and outward acceptance.[16] This ontology regards claims as

13. Menger, *Problems*, p. 214.

14. Max Alter, *Carl Menger and the Origins of Austrian Economics* (Boulder: Westview Press, 1990), p. 99.

15. *See* also Smith, *Austrian Philosophy*, pp. 301-302.

16. Reinach, p. 2.

a priori objects. That is, they come into being as a necessary consequence of certain acts or states of affairs:

> This a priori character does not mean anything dark or mystical, it is based
> on the simple facts which we have just mentioned: every state of affairs which
> is in the sense explained general and necessary is in our terminology *a
> priori*.[17]

The method described above, employed by Menger and Reinach, works essentially as follows: a) pick a legal or social object, and b) determine which states of affairs are necessary and sufficient conditions for that legal or social object to obtain. This method works only with those objects which we may know *a priori*. It cannot work with those objects which are purely positive, or the creations of human will.

3.21 Some Shortcomings of the Method from First Principles

Methodological individualism assumes our *a priori* knowledge of the nature of the objects which we seek to describe. In other words, we can grasp the necessary and general components of a claim without resort to anthropological or sociological study because we have *a priori* knowledge of claims. The necessary and general relations which comprise a claim are simply part of the nature of claims. It may well be the case that many objects of the positive law are in fact instantiations of objects for which we have *a priori* knowledge. Claims are a good candidate for this possibility. Contract law codifies many of the features of claims and obligations described by Reinach. It also seems to be the case that many codifications of contract law, although in different legal systems, nonetheless share many features. It may have been a daunting task to derive something even reasonably close to the exact theory of claims from a cross-cultural study of the law of claims. Reinach's approach seems to engender a quick and efficient means of describing *a priori* legal objects.[18] But for the applied legal ontologist, it is only a step in a larger process.

---

17. *Id.*, p. 5.
18. Moreover, it is the only exact method for doing so.

3.22 Only Part of the Job

To be precise, the approach from first principles fulfills the concerns expressed by principle II at the beginning of this chapter. The remaining four principles remain unfulfilled without more. To complete the job, an applied legal ontologist who has described a legal object correctly by means of the approach from first principles must now apply that ontology. The remaining steps are:

I.   An examination of the treatment of the legal object within existing legal systems, (for example, the law of contract);

III.   Determining whether existing legal systems employ the correct ontology, (that which is described by the approach from first principles);

IV.   If the existing legal ontology is incorrect, determining whether it results in problems such as economic inefficiencies or injustice;

V.   If the existing legal ontology results in inefficiency, injustice, or other societal woes, determining whether altering the law to reflect the correct ontology will avoid those woes.

Clearly, an approach from first principles is useful, for certain legal objects and to a certain extent, but a correct description of a legal ontology is only a beginning for the *applied* legal ontologist.

3.23 A Limited Realm of Inquiry

As mentioned above, the approach from first principles assumes that the legal object of one's study is one for which our knowledge is *a priori*. Reinach holds that a claim's existence is such that with or without the positive law (man-made codes) claims and

---

19. Reinach, p. 114.

obligations arise in the world as a necessary consequence of certain acts or states of affairs. Can the approach from first principles describe legal objects for which we do not have *a priori* knowledge? Clearly it cannot do so. By definition, positive law is the creation of human will and can indeed contradict the a priori law.

Any *enactment* is also properly called a *positive* law. The fact that enactments can contradict a priori law is what makes certain enactments unjust, and also indicates that enactments, as opposed to a priori law, cannot be approached by the method from first principles. The following are each enactments: a) "2 + 2 = 4", and b) "2 + 2 = 5". According to Reinach, the former enactment is "grounded" or "valid."[19] The latter is clearly invalid because it is not something which objectively ought to be.[20] The latter is, however, conceivably an enactment. Although the enactment "2 + 2 = 5" is something which we may comfortably say objectively ought not to be, other enactments may not necessarily share this quality. Examples of problem cases are such enactments as: "No parking," "Smoking is prohibited on domestic flights," or "Stopping is required at red lights." Such enactments are not so clearly grounded although they may comprise or reflect certain ontologies. Moreover, such ontologies may be confused or poorly elaborated. Applied ontology should be able to deal with legal objects and ontologies which are purely the creations of the positive law, yet the approach from first principles will not suffice for an examination of such enactments. Another approach must be utilized.

3.3 Empirical Studies

When laws are purely positive, having no a priori elements or features, the approach from first principles will fail. Yet legal objects which are purely positive should also be investigated from an ontological point of view. They may indeed comprise or compose an ontology which may or may not be flawed and which should be investigated. Ontological investigation of such laws is warranted by the five principles of applied legal ontology. Those five

---

20. *Ibid.*

principles also serve as a basis for an empirical method of legal ontology. Such a method follows the following basic formula which reflects the five principles set out at the beginning of this chapter:

(archeology)   I.   Choose a legal object and unravel its existing ontology (e.g., copyrightable things: expressions in various media, etc.).

(ontology)   II.   Determine whether the existing legal ontology of that object abides by principles of formal ontology and logic.

(evaluation)   III.   Determine, based on II, above, whether the existing legal ontology is correct.

(application)   IV.   If the law does not embody a correct ontology, determine what practical problems, injustices, or inefficiencies follow as a consequence of the incorrect ontology.

(adjustment)   V.   Determine how the law could be adjusted to reflect a correct ontology.

This method has all of the daunting interdisciplinary baggage associated with the complete five-part approach from first principles described above. It also adds the complication of unraveling the ontologies of objects whose existence may depend on historical developments taking place over hundreds of years. An example of this is patent law in the United States which owes its current form to a common law and statutory scheme which has evolved over the course of about 400 years in various legal systems.

3.31 History Is Important

Unlike *a priori* legal objects, unraveling the ontology of positive legal objects often requires an understanding of the history of their development. In the case of patent law, an understanding of history is crucial. Patent law itself arises out of two competing historical goals: a) promoting invention; and b) making inventive ideas available to the public. These goals have been expressed over time in various forms of statutory and common law patent protection. To fully understand the categories which have been created in the current U.S. patent scheme, the historical bases of U.S. and British patent laws must be explored.

3.32   *Legal Research, History, and the Common Law*

In the Anglo-American legal tradition, certain legal objects are created by enactments. Those enactments may be specifically located in time and space in that they have been passed by a legislature and signed by an executive on a certain date and at a specific place. Such statutes, rules, or regulations are examples of positive law-making. Yet there is another manner in which laws, which are typically just as enforceable as positive laws, may come into existence. The common law system, in which the judiciary discovers certain legal principles rather than the legislature or executive branch, has been responsible for much of the existing legal scheme which we take for granted. In order to properly describe the existing legal ontology of common-law legal objects, we must examine the development of the corresponding legal scheme through common law and statutes. In the following chapter, I will examine the existing legal ontology of intellectual property in this manner. Because cyberspatial entities have already been fitted into the legal categories of intellectual property, with contradictory results, we must first understand the existing legal ontology before criticizing it.

4

The Legal Ontology of Intellectual Property

In a written opinion for his decision in *Folsom v. Marsh*,[1] Justice Story stated that, "Patents and copyrights approach, nearer than any other class belonging to forensic discussion to what may be called the metaphysics of the law, where distinctions are, or at least may be, very subtle and refined, and, sometimes, almost evanescent."[2] It is surprising that this invitation to describe the metaphysics of intellectual property law has thus far not been accepted by philosophers. To understand the metaphysics of intellectual property law, a brief history of its development may be useful. There are three types of intellectual property and a separate course of development of the laws regarding each.

4.1 The Development of Patent Law

Before any laws were established to protect the rights of inventors to their inventions, a self-imposed monopoly of knowledge by inventors was the only means of protection available. Such a monopoly was maintained by a combination of secrecy and the inability of others to reverse-engineer new products.[3] As individual inventors became unable to sustain their monopoly of relevant knowledge pertaining to their inventions, and as others began to

---

1. (C.C.D. Mass. 1941) (No. 4901) Story, J.
2. *Ibid.*
3. Reverse-engineering is the process of figuring out how a device works by taking it apart and putting it back together. This is a process utilized now in the software industry among others.

43

discover how to reproduce secret products or processes, those with such knowledge came together in guilds to maintain their control of the market. At this time, there were still no legal means available to protect the rights of any individual or group's exclusive marketing of a product. Rather, members of guilds enforced their pacts with one another by either inviting potential competitors into the guilds or by using other tactics (such as force) to prevent competitors' entry into their markets.

In England, monopolies were first granted by the monarch in return for payments by the producers of goods. These "importation patents" were granted to foreigners who would bring new technologies. These foreign inventors would often be required to educate natives in the art for which their monopoly was granted and the patent lasted for a specific term of years. These monopolies were not given solely for inventions, but also for processes and crafts. In England, by the time of Queen Elizabeth, royal patents became disfavored because of what was seen as their tendency to stifle competition in a developing mercantile economy. Monopolies have long been understood to stifle competitiveness and upset free markets. Common law courts began to crack down on the most egregious abuses of the royal patents and eventually, in 1623, the Statute of Monopolies was passed to limit the Crown's ability to grant patents.[4]

In the American colonies, the antimonopolistic sentiment expressed by the Statute of Monopolies was reflected in laws passed in the colonies which restricted importation patents.[5] All of the colonies established their own patent systems which were well developed by the time of the American Revolution. However, the disparate systems made for little meaningful protection beyond state boundaries. Thus, at the Constitutional

---

4. In *The Clothworkers of Ipswitch,* Godbolt, 252 (Decided at Easter Term, 12 James I) (1614), the Court limited a patent granted by the King stating: "when that patent is expired, the king cannot make a new grant thereof; for when the trade has become common, and others have been bound apprentices to the same trade, there is no reason that such should be forbidden to use it." p. 254. (English Reports Full Reprint, Vol 78, p. 147.) The Statute of Monopolies: Statute 21, James I. Chapter 3.

5. For example, The General Court of Massachusetts, 1641: "There shall be no monopolies granted or allowed among us, but of such new inventions as are profitable to the country, and that for a short time."

Convention of 1787, a federal patent power was proposed by James Madison and Charles Pinckney and was adopted without debate as Article 1, Sec. 8, clause 8: "The Congress shall have power . . . to promote the progress of science and useful arts, by securing for limited times to authors and inventors the exclusive right to their respective writings and discoveries." By establishing the federal patent power and limiting its duration (patent rights currently last for only 20 years), the founders recognized the important incentive power of patents, but at the same time satisfied their strong antimonopolistic tendencies.

4.2   The Development of Trademark Law

Trademarks can be traced back to the practice of marking products produced by guild members. These marks served to identify the producers of goods and served as a method of advertisement. A guild mark also indicated that the product met the standards of quality necessary for guild membership. A marked product was thus preferred to an unmarked one. The common law of trademark developed first in England and then in the United States.[6] It arose originally to prevent manufacturers from trying to pass off their goods as someone else's. In this way, the grant of a right to a certain mark involved a recognition of the need to protect the good will which a manufacturer may develop in his customers.

In the United States, the individual states each developed their own trademark statutes before the first federal statutes were enacted in 1870 and 1876. The latter were declared unconstitutional in 1879 in the Supreme Court decision of *United States v. Stefans*.[7] The Supreme Court reasoned that, since no constitutional grant of federal authority over trademarks existed, the federal government could not usurp the power of the states to

---

6. Common law means simply that there was no law passed, but courts awarded those whose marks were infringed by others. The common law is court-made law. See Sidney A. Diamond, "The Historical Development of Trademarks," *The Trademark Reporter*, 65 (1975), p. 265.

7. 100 U.S. Reporter 82 (1879) (The U.S. Supreme Court Reporter—Official).

regulate in this area. Thus, in 1881 and 1905, the Congress enacted trademark laws based upon the federal power to regulate interstate trade. The current version of federal regulation of trademark, The Lanham Act, was passed in 1946. The Lanham Act does not recognize or create any new rights, it rather creates a mechanism whereby the common law of trademark may be enforced at the federal level.

4.3 The Development of Copyright Law

The law of copyright grew out of *de facto* monopolies which developed along with the establishment of presses. Publishers, much like guilds, sought to protect their roles as sole disseminators of information and kept the tools and other secrets of their trade to themselves. The publishers' motives were primarily economic. In the latter part of the seventeenth century, the Book Licensing Act was passed in Great Britain to be succeeded following its expiration in 1679 by the Statute of Anne in 1710. The Statute of Anne was established to grant authors and booksellers "the sole right and liberty of printing [books] for the term of one and twenty years." It is worthy of note that, until the early eighteenth century, publishers and bookbinders held more rights in an author's work than did the author. This state of affairs lasted until the American common law of copyright began to evolve greater rights for authors in their works whether published or not. Early versions of modern copyright law granted authors eternal rights to their unpublished works which then became limited upon the publication of the work, but modern statutory copyright grants authors' rights to the publication, reproduction and distribution of their expressions for the term of the author's lifetime plus seventy years.

The current U.S. federal law of copyright protection stems from the same clause of the Constitution which established the federal power over patents. This clause allows Congress to grant monopolies in expressions for a limited time period, just as the federal government may grant monopolies over the production of inventions for limited time periods.

4.4 The Diverse Subject Matter of Intellectual Property Law

As can be seen from the above brief histories of the development of the three main branches of intellectual property law, the laws themselves are most accurately considered to be the creations of the positive law rather than the recognition by courts of rights which may already have existed. Patents, trademarks, and copyrights, before the establishment of legal frameworks for their protection, were not recognized in any formal way. The development of these protections arose out of purely economic and practical reactions to the marketplace. The development of monopolies over ideas and concepts evolved, in the realms of copyright and patent, simply through the deliberate safeguarding of those ideas and methods. For expressions, authors and publishers enjoyed monopolies so far as they could maintain monopolies over the tools and means of production and distribution—in other words: *de facto* monopolies. Printing presses and binderies involved the use of specialized equipment and knowledge which could, for a period of time, be kept a secret from all but the most enterprising and wealthy competitors. When competitors emerged, it was often convenient for all possible competitors to enter into agreements amongst themselves to fend off further competition. This was true both for publishing houses and trade guilds.

The need for secrecy as the first historical weapon against economic competition in the production of goods and the dissemination of ideas points to the likely perception of inventions and expressions as having no innate protections, such as property rights in chattels, which inhered in other goods. The subject matter of each of the three areas of intellectual property law seem, however, to be slightly different.

4.41 The Scope of Patent Law

Modern federal patent law allows only for the award of patents to products, "compositions of matter," and processes or "new and useful" improvements of each of these. Specifically, "any new and useful process, machine, manufacture, or composition of matter, or any new and useful improvement thereof" may be patented.[8] Explicitly excluded from patent protection are ideas and "methods of operation" such as buttons on a video cassette recorder, or the pedals of a car.[9] Patents are typically thought of as applicable to "inventions" which are the applications of ideas rather than the ideas themselves. The distinction between an idea and the application of an idea is analogous to the distinction between the theory of gravity and a gravity-powered clock. The theory of gravity could not be patented, but its application in any particular invention may well be patented inasmuch as it results in a "new and useful" invention.

4.42 The Scope of Trademark Protection

Trademarks can only be registered for product names which are used in commerce. Modern trademark law also allows for the registration of marks used for services. Judge Friendly, in *Abercrombe & Fitch Co. v. Hunting World, Inc.*,[10] distinguished amongst four types of marks: 1) generic; 2) descriptive; 3) suggestive; and 4) arbitrary or fanciful. A generic or descriptive mark which has not acquired a "secondary meaning" may not be registered. Generic terms refer to the genus to which a product or service belongs, such as "Overnight Delivery, Inc." Generic terms such as this may never be granted trademark registration unless they have acquired, through use, some secondary meaning. Descriptive marks may be granted trademark protection so long as they are not deemed to be "deceptively misdescriptive." A descriptive mark might be "Speedy Delivery, Inc." Suggestive marks are partly descriptive and partly arbitrary or fanciful. They are descriptive of a product or service only through the use of one's imagination or perception (for instance "Lightning Delivery, Inc."). A fanciful mark has no connection between the mark used and the service or product. Fanciful marks are most readily granted protection. The only other bars to trademark registration are for geographic, immoral marks, national symbols, and names of living figures.[11]

---

8. U.S. Patent Act, Sec. 101.
9. *Gottschalk v. Benson,* 409 U.S. 63; *Parker v. Flook* 437 U.S. 584 (1978).
10. 537 F.2d 4 (1976).
11. 15 U.S.C. Secs. 1052 (a)–(d), (f).

Other types of marks that may issue are certification marks and collective marks. Certification marks indicate acceptance of a product or service by an organization, such as "AAA-approved." Collective marks indicate that the marketer or producer belongs to a group or organization such as "Upstate Milk Farmers." The owners of certification or collective marks are not the producers of the individual products, but rather the collective or certifying organization.

An interesting limitation on the subject matter of trademark protection is the requirement for the mark to serve primarily the purpose of identifying and distinguishing goods or services. The primary purpose test which is applied when a proposed mark is challenged, prevents the adoption by one of something which may be only a "trade dress." The shape of an aluminum can could be distinctive from that of all other aluminum cans used to package and preserve foods. Such a distinctive can, if designed primarily to distinguish and identify a product, may be awarded trademark protection. The shape of an aluminum can is the product's trade dress. A trade dress can only be granted trademark protection if its primary purpose is to distinguish and identify a particular product. Otherwise, a trade dress is not amenable to such protection. Recently, trademark protection has even been granted to particular, distinctive colors which have been found to serve the primary purpose of identifying and distinguishing a product from others.

As in patent law, there is a specific bar to trademark protection. The functional bar prohibits the registration of something as a trademark which serves a solely functional purpose. A feature of a product is considered functional if "it is essential to the use or purpose of the article or if it affects the cost or quality of the article."[12] Only those features which are primarily functional are barred from trademark protection.

4.43 The Scope of Copyright

The subject matter of copyright is original expressions. Although the Constitution only specifies that protection may be afforded to

---

12. *Inwood Laboratories, Inc. v. Ives Laboratories, Inc.*, 456 U.S. 844 (1982).

writings by authors, copyright protection has been extended to nearly every form of expression which may be contemplated, and which may be fixed in a "tangible medium." Originators of copyrighted materials hold the exclusive rights of reproduction, distribution, and first-sale. The first-sale doctrine recognized the right of a bona fide purchaser of an authorized reproduction to freely alienate his copy. Without the first-sale doctrine, used bookstores and the sales of used books would be illegal.

As with patent and trademark law, there are specifically barred subjects of copyright protection—most importantly, ideas. It is only the original expression of particular ideas that is prone to copyright protection, not the ideas themselves. Thus, for compilations of facts such as directories, maps, or charts, some original work on the part of the compiler must be present in order to afford such works copyright protection.[13] The law distinguishes between such compilations of facts and works containing original ideas. Two authors could compile exactly the same volumes of facts and, if the expressions of those facts are unique and original, their works may each be copyrightable. The only limitation is against actually copying the work of another author. For works containing ideas, as distinguished from bare facts, copyright is still only available if the expression of those ideas is original.

Copyright is not available for purely utilitarian works. However, copyright protection is available to those parts of a utilitarian work which serve an other-than-utilitarian purpose. Thus, in *Mazur v. Stein*,[14] copyright protection was granted to lamp bases which were in the form of statuettes although the lamps themselves were clearly utilitarian. Titles of works are also not granted copyright protection.

The current federal copyright statute indicates that protection "subsists . . . in original works of authorship fixed in any tangible medium of expression, now known or later developed."[15] This provision ensures that, as new media of expression develop, there is no confusion as to whether or not the expressions conveyed are susceptible to copyright protection. However, the term "tangible

---

13. *Schroeder v. William Morrow & Co.*, 566 F2d 3 (1977); *Amsterdam v. Triangle Publications, Inc.*, 189 F2d 104 (1951).

14. 347 U.S. 201 (1954).

15. 17 U.S.C. Sec.102(a).

medium of expression" is problematic in itself. An example of non-tangible and thus non-copyrightable expression is choreography. Without reducing a choreographed dance to some form of tangible medium (such as a film of the dance or choreographic notation), no copyright may obtain. This is true also of speeches, lectures, and other oral presentations.

It took an amendment of the Copyright Act to secure protection to computer programs which were previously held not to satisfy the "fixation" or "writing" requirements of copyright law.[16] The current limitation on obtaining copyright protection for software prohibits any protection for those elements of programs which lack sufficient originality and those elements which embody the only means of performing a certain function.

4.5   The Current Ontology of Intellectual Property Law

The law of intellectual property makes, in all of its branches, an important primary distinction between ideas, which are never the subject of exclusive rights, and other things which may be the subject of property rights. This distinction can be traced back to the roots of the various branches of intellectual property law. Intellectual property protection began simply through the deliberate keeping of secrets. Deliberate secret-keeping recognizes the tendency of ideas to spread once they become known or understood by others. Absent some common-law or statutory scheme protecting ideas, knowledge of another's ideas carries with it the ability, and presumably, the right to use that idea. One way in which ideas might be protected outside of an intellectual property scheme would be through contracts. Even now, contracts in the form of confidentiality agreements prevent individuals from using other persons' ideas. But a confidentiality agreement is only binding upon those who have entered the contract. Such an agreement will not protect against independent discovery of an idea.

---

16. 17 U.S.C. Sec. 117; compare *White-Smith Music Publishing Co. v. Apollo Co.,* 209 U.S. 1 (1908). Player piano rolls were not improperly reproduced because there was no fixed "writing" which could be directly perceived by others. This "direct perception" test is implicitly rejected by the amendment of the Copyright Act.

Thus, guilds, cooperatives, and other extra-legal relationships which may be entered into may guard against the spread of ideas to only a limited degree. Ideas are simply too hard to contain and prone to independent discovery.

What is somewhat easier to contain through legal structures and processes is the *application* of ideas, whether through products, processes, names, or expressions. Thus there have developed procedures for granting limited monopolies of patent, trademark, and copyright. The basic ontology of intellectual property consists of five types of things: ideas, products, processes, names and expressions. To comprehend the legal ontology of intellectual property, we must look first at each of these things.

4.51 Ideas

An understanding of the categorization of ideas in the legal context may best be achieved by looking at the distinctions drawn in the law of intellectual property between processes and ideas in patent law, and expressions and ideas in copyright law.

4.51.1 THE PROCESS/IDEA DISTINCTION IN PATENT LAW

There is a subtle but significant distinction drawn in patent law between processes, which are patentable, and ideas, which are not. As discussed above, patent protection is available for machines, manufactures, and compositions of matter, all of which are clearly physical entities. However, patents may also be granted for processes, which are not so clearly physical. How then do processes warrant the same degree of legal protection as machines, manufactures, and compositions of matter? Ideas may be thought of as preceding processes, which are the means toward the ends of machines, manufactures, and compositions of matter. For instance, the idea of a chemical substance would be expressed by a chemical formula or other model. The chemical formula is not patentable. However, the process of making the chemical substance *is* patentable and so may be the chemical itself as it is a composition of matter. One way to understand this fine distinction is by thinking of both the physical entities and processes which are patentable as being *applications* of abstract principles or ideas.

4.51.2 THE IDEA/EXPRESSION DICHOTOMY IN COPYRIGHT LAW

The dichotomy between ideas and expressions is similarly tricky to discern. One cannot copyright ideas, but only particular expressions of ideas. Moreover, the law distinguishes between ideas and information, neither of which may be the subject of copyright, and recognizes the need for differing degrees of originality in the expression of each before copyright protection is available. The degree of originality of the expression of information must be relatively high in order to warrant copyright protection, whereas that which is required for the expression of an idea may be lower. This is because facts or information are considered to be clearly a part of the public domain.

The courts in the U.S. have had to deal most directly with the idea/expression distinction in cases involving the copyrightability of forms—as in accounting, insurance, tax, or other business forms. In *Baker v. Selden*[17] the Supreme Court wrestled with the copyrightability of an accounting system. Selden claimed that Baker's accounting system infringed upon his copyright. The Court held that, since there had been no literal copying of Selden's forms, there was no infringement. The idea behind the accounting system was the "art" and was uncopyrightable, while the "description" of the art was all that was copyrightable.

The degree of protection which the courts have been willing to grant has also depended upon the range of variability possible in expressions of particular ideas. Thus, where forms for insurance or other contracts are concerned, because the ideas behind the forms are limited in variability, the courts have been wary of granting copyright protection.[18] In the case of the simplest forms, it could be argued that the idea and the expression of the idea are inseparable and thus no copyright would issue.

A curious and important caveat regarding the copyrightability of expressions is the requirement of "fixation" of an expression. The constitutional grant of copyright authority specifies that "writings" shall be afforded protection, but this has come to be interpreted as "any physical rendering of the fruits of creative,

---

17. 101 U.S. 99 (1879).
18. *See, e.g. Continental Casualty Co. v. Beardsly*, 253 F.2d 702 (1958).

intellectual or aesthetic labor."[19] Still, to be copyrighted, the fruits of that labor must have some physical fixation in some "tangible" medium. For instance, a speech or a musical performance is not copyrightable unless it is written down, or recorded on video or audio tape.

The extent to which sound recordings are considered copyrightable has been questioned for some time. Until 1972, due to the *White-Smith Music Publishing Co. v. Apollo Co.* case of 1908, neither performers nor producers could hold copyrights to sound recordings. In that case, player-piano rolls were determined not to be copies of the musical composition itself because they were not comprehensible to humans. Thus, it was not an infringement of copyright to make unauthorized reproductions of player-piano rolls. For similar reasons, it was believed that copyright could not extend to sound recordings. In an amendment to the Copyright Act in 1972, copyright protection was fully extended to sound recordings or "phonorecords."[20]

Even now, the scope of copyright protection available to sound recordings is somewhat more limited than that for other media of expression. For instance, owners of copyrights in sound recordings do not hold an exclusive right of performance, and others may reproduce and prepare derivative works short of actual, physical copies.[21]

The idea/expression dichotomy and idea/process distinctions are at the heart of the most basic limitations in intellectual property protection. In order to comprehend the distinctions between all of these various legal entities, we must look next to those which are afforded patent protection most easily—products.

4.52 Products

The legal category of products is less troublesome than the other four categories of things which may be afforded intellectual property protection. As discussed above, three sub-categories of products are deemed patentable: machines, manufactures, and compositions of matter. The only qualification for patentability of

---

19. *Goldstein v. California,* 412 U.S. 546 (1973).
20. 17 U.S.C. 102(a).
21. Copyright Act, Sec. 114.

any of these is that the product must be inventive. That is, it must not be naturally occurring and must be the result of some human artifice.

4.52.1 COMPOSITIONS OF MATTER

Even genetically engineered life forms are patentable given that they are compositions of matter created by human invention.[22] Because new life forms are man-made combinations of naturally-occurring materials, they are considered to be both manufactures and compositions of matter.[23] Compositions of matter are complexes of naturally occurring substances which are combined in an inventive way. To be patentable, a composition of matter must not be a naturally-occurring composition even though its parts may be.[24] Patents for new chemicals typically fall under this category. All of the constituent elements of a new chemical are not patentable even though the particular combination may be so. The justification for patentability of compositions of matter is that the inventor's discovery "is not nature's handiwork, but his own."[25]

4.52.2 MANUFACTURES

A manufacture is considered to be anything which is created by humans which is not otherwise naturally-occurring. Manufactures and other inventions are only patentable if they are also novel, nonobvious, and useful. A manufacture includes any physical good which may be used. Tools are manufactures even when they contain no moving parts.

4.52.3 MACHINES

Machines are manufactures with moving parts. They combine processes with manufactures. A machine is a complex manufacture.

---

22. *Diamond v. Chakrabarty,* 447 U.S. 303 (1980).
23. *Ibid.*
24. *Schering Corp. v. Gilbert,* 153 F.2d 428 (1946).
25. *Diamond v. Chakrabarty, supra.*

4.53 Processes

Processes are the only patentable subject matter which are not
themselves physical objects. Rather, they are ways of doing something. The clearest example of a patentable process would be one
whereby chemical elements or substances are combined using a
specific method in order to form another chemical or to otherwise
alter the original chemical. As long as the process is considered
inventive and nonobvious, then the inventor may obtain a patent
for that process. Non-patentable processes are typically so abstract
or general that they are akin to natural (or mathematical) laws.
For instance, a method of converting binary numbers to base ten
numbers which utilized simple mathematical algorithms was considered to be unpatentable by the Supreme Court in *Gottschalk v.
Benson.*[26]

4.54 Names

Names are a peculiar category to discuss in the ontology of intellectual property law. They are a distinct object of the law and are
afforded a fair amount of protection under the trademark scheme
discussed above in Section 3.42. They are also interesting because
the scope of trademark protection is limited by certain geographic
considerations. They are not a very problematic category for this
work, and are peripheral to the investigation of the ontology of
cyberspace. It is worth noting that they are afforded their own
ontological category in the law of intellectual property. The ontology of trademarks shall be explored more fully in a later work.

4.55 Expressions

The category of expressions is discussed in Section 4.43 above.
However, it is worth discussing here the scope of the rights that
may attach to expressions. Holders of copyrights have certain
exclusive rights to their expressions. They have: 1) an exclusive
right to reproduce their works; 2) an exclusive right to most deriv-

---

26. *Supra*, n. 9. However, mathematical processes may be patentable processes if they
are not deemed to be too general. Problems arise where the process is said to resemble the
idea behind it too closely.

ative works; 3) an exclusive right to distribute their works; and 4) an exclusive display right. Infringement of an author's reproduction and derivative work rights occurs whether the work is accessible to the public or not, while the latter three exclusive rights require some audience's perception for infringement to occur.[27]

A reproduction is a material object which, through either unaided perception, or the use of a machine, allows the original expression to be perceived, reproduced, or otherwise communicated.[28] Specific exceptions to the reproduction right include that which allows "transmitting organizations" to record a work for later broadcast as well as the right of software owners to make archival or other copies necessary for the proper operation of a program.[29]

The derivative right of a copyright holder protects non-literal, protectable elements of an expression. That is, works which utilize certain unique characters, plot structure, or other non-literal but original elements of another's expression may be considered to be derivative works and may infringe upon a copyright. There is a specific exception to this exclusive right which allows for parody.[30]

The performance right encompasses literary, musical, dramatic, motion picture, choreographic and audiovisual expressions.[31] Not covered by this right is the display of art works and sound recordings. The display right covers the display of art works and may include display through any developing technologies. Under the Copyright Act, the owner of a lawfully obtained copy has an unlimited right to display that copy, and only that copy, where it is located.[32] Thus, the owner may not make copies of his copy and may not display that copy via broadcast to other locations. He may display only "one image at a time, to viewers present at the place where the copy is located."[33]

---

27. *See* 17 U.S.C. 101. Display must be to a "substantial number of persons."
28. 17 U.S.C. Sec. 101.
29. 17 U.S.C. Sec. 117.
30. *Ibid.*
31. 17 U.S.C. Sec. 106(4). Of course, this provision is not so easily applied to the problem of display over networks. A web page remains at the place it is located even when browsed remotely, although a *reproduction* of that page is made on the browser's computer.
32. 17 U.S.C. Sec. 109(b).
33. *Ibid.* This caveat is especially problematic in cyberspace which is not clearly a broadcast medium.

4.6 The Categories of Intellectual Property Law

The above constitutes the basic categorization of legal objects made in the law of intellectual property in the United States. What remains to be seen is the way in which computer-mediated phenomena fit into this categorical scheme, and whether this scheme is sufficient or flawed. The categories available are:

expressions

inventions (machines, processes, products)

These categories do not exhaust all the categories of intellectual property law. Trademarks protect names to limited degrees. The law itself has recognized that new types of machines, processes, methods, and expressions are being invented and utilized all of the time. Some purposeful vagueness exists in the law to cover newly-developed media of expression. Computer-mediated phenomena have been difficult to categorize, and often seem to fall in more than one category at a time. The following chapter will explore the law of intellectual property as it has been applied to computer-mediated phenomena and I will attempt to discern the problems associated with the legal categorization to date.

5

The Legal Ontology
of Software

The development of software was not contemplated by the
drafters of the first Copyright Act, and it was left to the courts to
fit software into the existing intellectual property scheme until the
Copyright Act's amendment in 1976.[1] To date, there are only a
handful of legal decisions regarding the Internet or other computerized phenomena. All computer-mediated phenomena involve
software at some level. In the preceding chapter I set forth the
current ontology of the law of intellectual property. That ontology has been applied by extension to the developing law of software inasmuch as software has been treated as a type of
intellectual property.

Software is defined in the *Data Processing Glossary* as "everything that is not hardware [relating to a computer]. [Hardware is]
physical equipment used in data processing."[2] The statutory definition of software is: "a set of instructions to be used in a computer in order to bring about a certain result."[3] Both of these
definitions are unsatisfactory because they fail to account for software's unusual property of being able to exist in the form of hardware. That is, the instructions which may be programmed into a
microprocessor, may also be "hardwired" into a microprocessor.
The statutory definition at least does not rule out this possibility,
but jurists have, for lack of an adequate understanding of software, had difficulties in dealing with software's peculiar nature.

Because software may be "hardwired"[4] into microprocessors

---

1. *Supra*, Chapter 4, n. 16.
2. Science Research Association, Inc.: 1979.
3. 17 U.S.C. Sec. 101: *See, Apple Computer, Inc. v. Franklin Computer Corporation*,
714 F.2d 1240, 1252 (3d Cir. 1983).

the U.S. courts have sometimes treated software like machines, which may be thought of as hardwired to perform certain tasks. Machines are, of course, the typical subject of patent law. Software has also been treated by U.S. courts as though it were a matter of expression—the typical subject of copyright law. By trying to fit software into one or the other of these categories, the U.S. courts and legislature have had to alter their interpretations of the ontology of intellectual property law for which expressions, machines, and processes have, until now, enjoyed a fairly clear distinction from one another. The difficulty faced by the courts in dealing with software as a type of intellectual property may indicate that the existing ontology of intellectual property must be re-evaluated. Before addressing this possibility, I now set forth a thorough outline of the current legal status of software.

5.1 Software and Patents

Software has been around at least since the invention of digital computers over 50 years ago. Before the invention of magnetic and optical media for information storage, software was stored on punch cards resembling the player-piano rolls of the nineteenth century. In the sense that both player-piano rolls and punch cards carried instructions which machines carried out, player-piano rolls were software of a sort. Before even player-piano rolls, the Jacquard loom ran on software. Weavers who operated manual looms also used software to operate their looms and make pre-determined patterns. The software which loom operators worked from looked something like Figure 5.1:

---

4. Microchips are collections of switches which may be either on or off. By introducing software to RAM, or programmable switches, the switches are set up by the software to be either on or off in patterns which direct input toward certain output. RAM may be re-programmed in that the switches are reset either by turning off the current to the microchip, or by re-introducing code to the switches. Microchips may also be hardwired with certain programming such that the switches are either on or off in preset patterns, just as they might be if programmed that way. Such ROM may not be reprogrammed.

FIGURE 5.1

X			X			X		X	
	X		X		X		X		X
X		X			X			X	

Patterns like the one above indicated to the operator of a loom the manner in which to use the pedals and when to throw the shuttle cock. The complexity of the pattern depended upon the capabilities of the loom, some of which had eight pedals or more. The Jacquard loom used punch cards to automate this process by eliminating the need for human pedaling. There is no case law regarding the copyrightability of loom software, but a pivotal case regarding player-piano rolls affected the copyrightability of computer software for about 70 years.

Until the 1976 amendment of the Copyright Act, computer programs were outside the scope of copyright protection based upon the reasoning of *White-Smith Music Publishing Co. v. Apollo Co.*[5] The Supreme Court held that, since the expressions contained in player-piano rolls were not directly perceptible by humans and because the underlying works could not be directly reproduced without the aid of a machine (a player-piano), the rolls were deemed not to be amenable to copyright protection. The Court reasoned that no protectable expression existed where the information made no sense to a human's direct perception. One could not "read" a player piano roll without the aid of a machine. The same held true for computer software. This so-called "direct-perception test" was rejected by those who drafted the 1976 amendment of the Copyright Act. Before this amendment various courts had toyed with the notion of applying patent protection to software.

In the early days of computer programming, university students and professors would freely exchange code to run on their time-shared computers.[6] There was no marketing of software and

---

5. 209 U.S. 1, 28 S.Ct 319 (1908).
6. For an excellent history of programming, *see*, generally, Stephen Levy, *Hackers* (New York: Anchor Press/Doubleday, 1984). Before personal computers, university main

those with access to computers were mostly eager for the opportunity to use them and make them do things. Hackers on these machines exchanged their programs freely as a matter of pride in their creations. When the first personal computers emerged on the market, programmers began to seek more than simply moral rewards for their efforts. An example is the copyright of the MS-DOS operating system by Bill Gates who, in 1975, complained about "hobbyists" who were "ripping off" his software.[7] By the time personal computers were available to the general public, the issue of the patentability of software had already been litigated in the U.S. Supreme Court. In *Gottschalk v. Benson*[8] the Court ruled against the legitimacy of a patent claim for a method of converting binary-coded decimal numbers into pure binary numbers by way of software. The Court held that the patent claim was invalid because it would have effectively pre-empted the use of a mathematical algorithm which the Court reasoned was the same as a mathematical formula and thus a law of nature.[9] But the decision did not completely foreclose the possibility of software patents:

> It is said that the decision precludes a patent for any program servicing a computer. We do not so hold . . . What we come down to in a nutshell is the following.
>
> It is conceded that one may not patent an idea. But in practical effect that would be the result if the formula for converting BCD numerals to pure binary numerals were patented in this case . . . the patent would wholly pre-empt the mathematical formula and in practical effect would be a patent on the algorithm itself.[10]

In reaching this decision, the Court defined an algorithm as "[a] procedure for solving a given type of mathematical problem

---

frames were the tools upon which computer programmers learned and honed their skills. Students and faculty shared time on these mainframes because they were so expensive and their resources were relatively scarce.

7. See Paul Freiberger and Michael Swaine, *Fire in the Valley: The Making of the Personal Computer* (1984), 169. Ironically, Gates himself had bought the code which was the foundation for MS-DOS from someone else for a pittance compared with what it has earned him.

8. 409 U.S. 63 (1972).

9. *Ibid.*, p. 67.

10. *Ibid.*, pp. 71–72.

. . ." and that definition has stuck in the law of patents and software ever since.[11]

An algorithm is not a formula. An algorithm is defined as: "any method of computation, whether algebraic or numerical, or . . . any method of computation consisting of a comparatively small number of steps. . . [i]n computer terminology, an algorithm is a detailed logical procedure which represents the solution of a particular problem."[12] A formula is not an algorithm. Rather, a formula in mathematics and physics is a statement expressed in symbols of a relationship between quantities. For instance, $e = mc^2$ is a formula expressing the relationship of energy to mass. While a formula represents a law of nature, an algorithm does not necessarily do so.

In 1978, the Supreme Court again addressed the issue of software patentability in *Parker v. Flook*.[13] The patent application in *Flook* included an algorithm for the computation of alarm limits of various emissions from catalytic converters.[14] The Court rejected the application holding that it included subject matter which was inappropriate for granting a patent—namely, the algorithm. While Justice Stevens, writing for the majority, admitted that the algorithm which was part of the application would not wholly preempt the use of the mathematical *formula* underlying the algorithm, he nonetheless equated a patent for the algorithm, upon which the patent application relied, with a patent for the formula $2\pi r$. Both the algorithm claimed and the formula for the circumference of a circle, were algorithms according to Stevens:

> Respondent's application simply provides a new and presumably better method for calculating alarm limit values. If we assume that method was also known . . ., then respondent's claim is, in effect, comparable to a claim that the formula $2\pi r$ can be usefully applied in determining the circumference of a wheel . . . Very simply, our holding today is that a claim for an improved method of calculation, even when tied to a specific end use, is unpatentable subject matter under Sec. 101 [of the patent law].[15]

11. *Ibid.*, p. 65.
12. *Von Nostrand's Scientific Encyclopedia* (Fifth Edition), p. 87.
13. 437 U.S. 584 (1978).
14. *Ibid.*, 585–86.
15. *Ibid.*, 594–95, n. 18.

Despite both *Benson* and *Flook*, the Supreme Court refused to rule out the possibility of granting patents to software, a fact acknowledged in *Benson* and by the United States Court of Customs and Patent Appeals in *Application of Freeman*.[16] The Court in that case stated that there was a possibility of granting patents to software, although it did not do so.

In *Diamond v. Diehr*,[17] the Supreme Court continued to disallow patents for claims[18] which consisted of mathematical algorithms. The Court held that such claims were laws of nature and thus inappropriate subject matter for patent protection.[19] The claims in the patent application in *Diamond v. Diehr* were for a process for curing synthetic rubber and included the use of a mathematical formula. The Court allowed a patent to issue in this case even though the disputed claims involved algorithms applied to computers. Justice Rehnquist argued that the patent application was for an entire industrial process of which a mathematical formula (which he mistakenly conflates with an algorithm) was but a part. The Court concluded that, as distinguished from *Benson* and *Flook*, in which the patent applications were for nothing more than mathematical formulae, "[i]n contrast, the respondents here do not seek to patent a mathematical formula. Instead, they seek patent protection for a process of curing synthetic rubber. Their process admittedly employs a well-known mathematical equation, but they do not seek to preempt the use of that equation."[20]

With this line of cases, from *Benson* and *Flook* to *Diehr*, the Supreme Court has distinguished between mathematical or natural laws expressed in symbolic form and those same laws as applied in a machine or a process. Software patent applications are now routinely granted. The current analysis undertaken in analyz-

---

16. 73 F2d 1237, 1244 (1978). This Court no longer exists.

17. 450 U.S. 175 (1981).

18. The parts of patent applications which are called "claims" consist of detailed descriptions of every part and process for which the patent application is sought. A machine, for instance, may consist of new and original parts and processes for which a patent might be granted which would foreclose the use of those parts and processes by others. A machine may also consist of old parts, used in other machines, but use new processes, or vice versa. Patent protection will only be granted for those aspects (claims) of a patent application which are new and inventive.

19. *Ibid*. at 185–86.

20. *Ibid*.

ing a software patent application involves first asking whether the claim either directly or indirectly recites a mathematical formula and then inquiring into whether the claimed invention amounts to nothing more than that formula. If the formula fulfills only a functional role in the claimed invention, then a patent may issue, otherwise the claim will be rejected as prohibited subject matter.[21] A growing number of software patents are being issued now as software authors learn how to word their claims correctly to get them through this test.[22]

5.2 Software and Copyrights

It is well settled that copyright law protects all forms of computer software.[23] For software authors, copyright seems a natural vehicle for protection of their authorship rights. Copyright was the first, and remains the most widely used, method of intellectual property protection for software, although patent is catching up lately.[24] What has remained problematic in the field of software copyright is the fact that software has many different levels of possible originality and authorship. Thus, it is often difficult to prove that copyright infringement of software has occurred.

Software typically begins with source code, or that code which is "written" by the programmer. The source code is often written in a "higher-level" language than that of the object code which is implemented by the computer. The source code is typically decipherable by other computer programmers so that the program flow can be understood by a careful reading of the source code.

---

21. *See*, e.g. *Arrhythmia Research Technology v. Corazonix Corp.*, 958 F2d 1053 (Fed. Cir. 1992), 1058.

22. *See* Dan L. Burk, "Patents in Cyberspace: Territoriality and Infringement on Global Computer Networks," *Tulane Law Review*, 68 (1993), p. 31.

23. *See*, for example, *Stern Electronics v. Kaufman*, 669 F.2d 852 (2.d Cir. 1982) (source code is a protectable literary work); *Williams Electronics, Inc. v. Arctic International, Inc.*, 685 F.2d 870 (3d Cir. 1982) (programs stored on ROM are prone to copyright protection); *CGA Corp. v. Raymond Chance*, 217 U.S. Patent Quarterly, 718 (N.D. Cal. 1982) (object code is protected by copyright).

24. Copyright protects for longer periods of time (the life of the author plus 70 years) but patent protection is stronger, granting a total monopoly in the protected art. Patent infringement is punished more severely and defending a patent infringement suit is more costly.

The source code is typically compiled by use of a compiling program and is turned into the object code which is indecipherable by most humans.

The non-literal elements of software are many. Non-literal elements of literary works include unique characters and settings for which an author may acquire some copyright protection. Non-literal elements of software may include such things as a program's structure, its purpose or intended use, and the look and feel of the software when used. The difficulty of determining copyright infringement of software is in part due to the many different levels of expression involved in any single piece of software. These levels of expression include: the code itself (both source and object), the program's structure, its purpose, and its look and feel when run. The difficulty posed by determining infringement at these many different levels has resulted in the formation of an exception in the law of copyright when applied to software.

Ordinarily, the courts have used what is called the "ordinary observer test" to determine whether a copyrighted work's literal or non-literal elements have been infringed by another work. Thus when one work bears a substantial similarity to another, a similarity which would be clear in the eyes of an "ordinary observer," the later-produced work must be deemed to be infringing.[25]

But at some levels of the expression involved in computer software, the ordinary observer test is impractical—namely, where the source and object codes are concerned. The ordinary observer may not detect substantial similarities between the source or object codes of substantially similar software because an ordinary observer would not likely understand those elements of a program. The courts have therefore taken away part of the jury's function by allowing the use of expert testimony to determine substantial similarity between those elements of a program's expression which are typically beyond the ken of the ordinary observer.[26]

---

25. See *Whelan Associates, Inc. v. Jaslow Dental Laboratory,* 797 F2d 1222 (3d Cir. 1986), *cert denied* 107 S.Ct 877 (1987). This presumption can be overcome by proof that the second work was produced independently of the first.
26. *Ibid.*

The Copyright Act of 1976 expressly extends protection by copyright to all literary works including software.[27] Thus, all of the protection afforded to other literary works is afforded to software, including protection of all nonliteral elements of expression discussed above. For works of authorship such as novels, the non-literal elements which are covered by copyright include unique plot structures, settings, or characters.[28] The question which has perplexed the courts has been the distinction between the non-literal elements of software and the *ideas* inherent in the software. This distinction is important because of the idea/expression dichotomy in the law of copyright. This dichotomy is expressed as follows:

> In no case does copyright protection for an original work of authorship extend to any idea, procedure, process, system, method of operation, concept, principle, or discovery, regardless of the form in which it is described, explained, illustrated, or embodied in such work.[29]

This dichotomy reflects the same ontology which prohibits patent protection of bare ideas, in other words, of ideas unembodied in any physical invention or process.

The idea/expression dichotomy was put to a test a century ago by the Supreme Court. The Court stated that the purpose or function of a utilitarian work[30] is the idea of that work. Everything which is unnecessary to the purpose or function of a utilitarian work is considered to be the copyrightable expression.[31] Thus, wherever there exists more than one way to fulfill a particular purpose or function, the courts may decide that the particular means used to perform that function constitutes expression. This reasoning extends copyright protection to nearly every level of expression inherent in a computer program.[32]

---

27. *Ibid.*
28. *See*, e.g. *Twentieth-Century Fox Film Corp. v. MCA, Inc.*, 715 F.2d 1327, 1329 (9th Cir. 1983).
29. 17 U.S.C. Sec. 102(b) (1982).
30. Like instructions for programming a VCR, or a recipe for stew.
31. *Baker v. Selden*, 101 U.S. (11 Otto) 99 (1879).
32. *See Whelan, supra*, n. 25.

The *idea* of a piece of software, or the non-copyrightable elements, seems now to be restricted to the most general purpose or function of that software. One cannot copyright the general idea of a word-processing program or of a spreadsheet program, as each of these ideas is a function or purpose. Much litigation now centers upon the infringement of the "look and feel" of pieces of software. Part of the drive to patent software has been the desire to avoid the messy evidentiary questions posed in copyright infringement cases regarding the "look and feel" of potentially infringing software. As patents protect the code itself, the look and feel of similar pieces of software would be irrelevant to questions of patent infringement.

5.21 *Problems of Exclusive Rights in Software Copyrights*

Other problems arise, however, with regard to copyright protection of software. These problems relate to the various exclusive rights which copyright owners have. These exclusive rights include those of reproduction, distribution, and first-sale. The nature of software and its interaction with hardware has required a unique interpretation of each of these rights. This is because, unlike other forms of expression, software is readily copied and the exclusive rights of software authors are more easily prone to infringement than are those of authors in most other media. For instance, it is usually prohibitively expensive to photocopy whole novels for illicit sales of unauthorized reproductions. Such "pirated" books are also easy to spot due to their degraded quality. Moreover, many pieces of software *require* making copies of the originals which are purchased legally. Most software distributed now, for instance, must be "installed" onto a computer-owner's hard-drive in order to use that software. Such installation would be regarded as a reproduction of the original without certain exceptions which were carved out of the existing Copyright Act.

New rules have emerged regarding the reproduction, distribution, and first-sale of software. Under the current Copyright Act, an owner of copyrighted software may make archival copies or adaptations of software which may be necessary to enable the program to run on his computer. Software purchasers may also sell the originals of their lawfully-obtained software, but may not rent or lease them to others. This exception recognizes the ease with which a renter of software may make illicit copies.[33] Ordinarily, the so-called "first-sale" doctrine allows the owners of copyrighted works to dispose of them as they will, including by renting or leasing books or other works which they may own. The copyright holder's distribution rights are restricted to the first-sale of the work.[34] The making of archival copies of software is simply a recognition of the frequency of crashed hard-drives or ruined original disks. The installation of software onto hard-drives is a specifically recognized exception to the exclusive reproduction right held by the author.

These exceptions recognize that software is reproduced necessarily as part of its very functioning. Software is reproduced in the memory of a computer in order to function. This reproduction is statutorily recognized as within the software owner's (purchaser's) rights.[35] These exceptions were built into the Computer Software Copyright Act of 1980 as a result of the unique nature of software as opposed to other works of authorship.

5.22 *The Idea/Expression Dichotomy in Software Copyright*

Most litigation in the U.S. regarding software copyrights has been over the dichotomy between ideas and expressions. While the decision in *Whelan*[36] seems to have made almost every element of software prone to copyright protection, other jurisdictions have been more restrictive. The Fifth Circuit Court of Appeals in Texas has held that such non-literal elements as the structure, sequence, and organization of software may be part of the *idea* of the program and thus not be amenable to copyright.[37] The Ninth Circuit court of Appeals has held that the determination of which elements are ideas and which are expressions turns on the particular facts of each case, leaving the question essentially open.[38]

---

33. 17 U.S.C. Sec. 117; See *Step-Saver Data Systems, Inc. v. Wyse Technology,* 939 F.2d 91, 96 (3d Cir. 1991), n. 7.

34. 17 U.S.C. Sec 109(a).

35. 17 U.S.C. Sec 106(1), 501(a); *See also Vault Corporation v. Quaid Software Limited,* 847 F.2d 255 (5th Cir. 1988).

36. *Supra,* n. 125.

37. *Plains Cotton Coop. Assn. v. Goodpasture Computer Serv., Inc.,* 807 F.2d 1256 (5th Cir. 1987).

38. *Johnson Controls, Inc. v. Phoenix Control Systems, Inc.,* 886 F2.d 1173 (9th Cir. 1989).

Recently, the extent to which copyright may protect software was before the Supreme Court in *Lotus Development Corp. v. Borland International, Inc.*[39] Lotus initially sued Borland in 1990 over the menu system used by Borland in its Quattro spreadsheet program. Lotus claimed that Quattro's pulldown menus infringed upon their copyrighted Lotus 1-2-3 spreadsheet. The trial court agreed with Lotus, but the Federal Appeals court in Boston held that the menu system was not an expression but a "method of operation" for which no copyright was available. The appellate judge likened the menu system to the buttons on a video cassette recorder.[40] Methods of operation are specifically excluded from copyright protection under the Copyright Act. The Supreme Court recently refused to overturn the Appellate Court decision.

Clearly, software has fit uncomfortably into the Copyright Act, requiring some modifications in the Act itself to accommodate software's peculiar qualities. The strangest accommodation is embodied in the Semiconductor Chip Protection Act (SCPA), which extends the Copyright Act's protections to the hardware upon which software works. Although copyright has traditionally not been available to utilitarian goods, the SCPA makes an exception in the case of computer chips.

5.23 *The SCPA: Copyright Protection for Computer Chips*

Computer chips are reproduced through a sort of photographic process by which various layers of the chip's topography are chemically etched out of silicon wafers in patterns that are embodied in "mask works." Mask works are like photographic negatives of various parts of the chips' circuitry. The SCPA protects mask works for computer chips from being copied. Excluded from the SCPA is protection for "procedure, process, system, method of operation, concept, principle, or discoveries." In other words, the act protects only the structure of the chips as embodied in the mask works, but not the way in which the final chips function.[41] These exclusions mirror other exclusions from copyright protection.

---

39. 73 F.3d 355 (1st Cir. 1995).
40. See "Court to Ponder Copyright laws for Software," *Wall Street Journal* 9/28/95, B1.
41. 17 U.S.C. Sec 902 *et seq.*

The SCPA also protects mask work owners' exclusive reproduction and distribution rights. Unlike copyright, however, the
exclusive rights to mask works last only ten years as compared
with the period of the author's lifetime plus 70 years otherwise
available for copyrighted works.[42] The implications of the
Semiconductor Chip Protection Act are strange considering that a
mask work may be used to produce ROMs which are, as
described earlier, chips into which software is hardwired. This
opens up yet another avenue of protection for software not available to any other type of copyrightable work.

5.3 Analysis of the Current Legal Ontology of Software

As it stands right now, the legal ontology of software is anything
but clearly defined. Unlike any other legal object, the law continues to consider software amenable to two very different and
mutually exclusive categories of legal protection: namely copyright and patent. The ontology that results is consequently both
confused and confusing. Figure 5.2 on the following page depicts
the various categories available for software and their status under
the law of patent and copyright:

Clearly, the problem areas in this tree (highlighted) result from
the vagueness of the boundaries between ideas and expressions or
between ideas and algorithms when software is at issue. What is
the distinction between idea and expression, and why is this distinction so problematic in the present context?

5.4 Idea vs. Expression

The dichotomies between ideas and expressions, in copyright law,
and ideas and algorithms in patent law, did not become particularly problematic until lawmakers and jurists sought to extend the
law of intellectual property to software. Typically, it is not difficult
to discern the divergence of idea and expression in literary and
other works. Consider James Joyce's *Ulysses*. The idea of the book
is taking an ordinary day in the life of a rather ordinary man

---

42. *Ibid.*

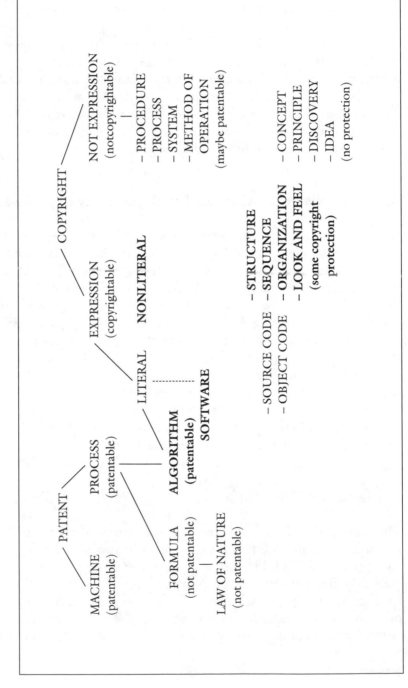

FIGURE 5.2

(Leopold Bloom) and making it into an epic reminiscent of Greek drama. This idea is clearly not a copyrightable element of *Ulysses* even if the work as a whole is protected by copyright. The particular situations and characters in *Ulysses* are part of the *expression* of that idea. Stephen Daedelus's drunken rage in the whorehouse is a protectable expression inasmuch as he carries out particular acts such as raising his walking stick and shattering a lamp in the process and uttering certain things simultaneously.

It is up to the trier of fact to find whether two expressions are *substantially similar* to a degree that one is an infringement upon the other. Drunken rages in whorehouses in general are not protectable. It is the particular attributes of a story, such as characters in specific situations, that are protectable expressions of underlying ideas. The dialogue spoken by characters is certainly protectable expression. The description of a scene is also certainly protectable expression. Two authors may describe Big Ben although Big Ben's attributes are more or less constant. Each author's description is protectable expression while the idea of Big Ben, or the idea of describing Big Ben, is not protectable.

Implicit in the scheme of intellectual property law is the assumption that there are an infinite number of possible ways to express a single idea. If this were not the case, then there would be a limited number of possibly copyrightable descriptions of Big Ben, or stories about average days in the lives of average men. It has never been the purpose of intellectual property law to limit the number of creative works. In fact, the purpose of copyright is to promote creative works. By granting protection for authors over the works which they produce, the copyright law provides a profit incentive for authors to create more works. Like patents, copyrights extend a limited monopoly over the fruits of creation. The copyright scheme's monopoly lasts a relatively long time—throughout the author's lifetime plus an extra 70 years. Such a monopoly would hinder the creation of works of authorship were it not for the fact that any single idea may be expressed in an infinite number of ways. At any one time, every author should be able to describe Big Ben in the course of his novels or poetry without having to worry about the infringement of a copyright. The extent of copyright protection afforded to authors is based upon an assumption that no two authors will express the same idea in exactly the same way.

The basic plot of every murder mystery is that some number of people are killed and the hero or heroine must discover who the murderer is. This is clearly an idea. The number of particular expressions of that idea is also nearly unlimited given the sheer number of murder mysteries there are. The difference between idea and expression has not been a point of much contention where written and other artistic works have been concerned because it is frankly not a very difficult task to discern copyright infringement for most traditional media. The ordinary observer test is easily applied to movies, books, music and plays. When, to an ordinary observer, one work bears a "substantial similarity" to another, the presumption is that the later work is an infringement of the earlier.

The dichotomy between algorithms and formulas in patent law is a somewhat more difficult matter as far as evidentiary proof in litigation. The principle which undergirds this distinction is the same, however, as that which is behind the dichotomy between ideas and expressions in copyright law. Again, patent law grants a limited monopoly for the fruits of creative labor. But while the patent monopoly is currently only 20 years, the tension between the goals of encouraging invention and not restricting competition have forced distinctions between formulae and algorithms to be drawn. The assumption behind the dichotomy between algorithms and formulae is that for every result to be obtained through computation, there is an unlimited number of possible algorithms which may be used to derive that result. Thus, formulae may not be protected, but algorithms may be. The formula for calculating force (force = mass × acceleration) is unprotectable because it is not a method of calculation, but an expression of a natural fact or a relation between quantities.

5.5 The Peculiar Nature of Software

Software appears to be a very different sort of thing than novels or machines. Essential to an understanding of the sources of difficulty in applying the laws of copyright or patent to software is an understanding of commonsense differences amongst software, novels, and machines.

The above has been an attempt to explain how the law of intellectual property, which embodies a certain ontology, has been applied to software so far with dubious success. The distinctions drawn within the law of intellectual property among ideas, expressions, algorithms, and formulae may well hold for traditional media, but they have been difficult for courts to apply to computer-mediated phenomena.

Software seems to be a type of hybrid object somewhere between expression and process or machine. In the next chapter, I will move away from discussing the law and begin and examination of the commonsense ontology of software.

6

The Commonsense Categories
of Cyberspace

The commonsense ontology of cyberspace must offer methods by which, without much in the way of philosophical analysis, the objects of cyberspace may be rationally categorized. A commonsense ontology is nothing more than a categorization of objects which ordinary people might be apt to make. As discussed earlier, we engage in a commonsense ontology all of the time. The law embodies many crucial commonsense categories. For instance, real property is distinct from chattels and intellectual property, and each is treated distinctly pursuant to separate legal schemes. Whether or not this categorization embodies a commonsense ontological distinction is a question that must be analyzed by relating the method and matter of that distinction to commonsense understandings of other, similar distinctions in the world at large. This is how a commonsense ontology differs from an ontology of the commonsense world. The world at large contains a multitude of objects which we might not consider to be commonsense objects or part of the commonsense world. For instance, probability wave-packets are not a commonsense object, but they are objects in the world at large which may be accounted for in a commonsense ontology of the world. In other words, even though an object might be outside of the realm of what we might consider to be commonsense objects (or those objects which are believed to exist by common consent), any object may still fit into a commonsense ontology of things in general. Even though a wave-packet is not a commonsense object in the sense that it is not something which is believed to exist by common consent, it may still fit into a categorization of objects which includes the category of intelligible objects, where this category includes everything which may be thought of existing.

77

An essential first step in devising a commonsense ontology is the process of deciding what shall be included in a final ontology. An ontology which is to include every possible object might start with the following basic categories: intelligible and sensible. Every object which may be thought of will fit into one of these two categories. A ukulele is both an intelligible and a sensible object in that it may be thought of and it may be perceived, held, and played. A unicorn is an intelligible object which, although it does not inhabit the real world, may nonetheless be thought of. Further categories of sensible objects include the commonsense categories: animal, vegetable, mineral, and so forth. Ordinary people employ this sort of categorization and a commonsense ontology of cyberspace should do likewise.

6.1   The Parts of Cyberspace

All computer-mediated phenomena are sensible. Each aspect of cyberspace may be experienced. The following is a classification of those sensible components which currently comprise computer-mediated phenomena.

6.11   Bits (BInary digiTS)

The term "bit" is short for "binary digit" and is the smallest unit of information. Computers which employ binary logic consist of switches which may be in one of two states. Each of these states is a bit. All digital computers, including mechanical, electrical, and those yet to be developed (biological? quantum?) share the fact that the smallest unit of information which they may manipulate is a bit. In binary mathematics, bits are represented by the numerals "0" and "1". The transistors in the silicon chips of modern digital computers store bits by switching between two different voltage states, high and low. The bit is the fundamental unit of cyberspace and, inasmuch as most computing is carried out by digital rather than analog[1] computers, bits are essential to every aspect of computer-mediated phenomena in general.

---

1. All of our perceptions are of analog information. Spectra are an example of analog information. Most things which we perceive fall somewhere on a continuum and not as either ones or zeroes, on or off. All of the information between zero and one is analog.

6.12 Bytes

A byte is a group of bits which is operated on by a computer as a unit. In most personal computers, a byte is composed of eight bits, which is a convenient number for representing alphanumeric characters. The American Standard Code for Information Interchange (ASCII) is an example of an alphanumeric character set whose individual characters are each represented by a different byte. Bytes are the smallest units of computation in that the processing of information by digital computers typically occurs through the manipulation of bytes or strings of bytes.

6.13 Words

Words are another unit of cyberspace and words too are composed of bits. At one time, computers were typically either word-oriented or byte-oriented and handled information as either bytes or words. Now, most computers use a combination of words and bytes. Words may be composed of varied numbers of bytes. A word is an ordered group of characters or bits which occupies a storage location of a computer as a unit.

6.14 Algorithms

An algorithm is a detailed mathematical or logical procedure for solving a problem. Algorithms are used in computer programs and involve the solutions, through discrete mathematical or logical steps, of mathematical or logical problems. Algorithms are also used by humans in such everyday activities as cooking dinner or driving a car.

6.15 Programs

Computer programs may consist of one or several algorithms and are the complete set of instructions and data used to direct a computer to perform a certain function. Any piece of software is a program. Types of programs include: programming languages, by which programs are written, and operating systems, (like MS-DOS or Windows) which generate interfaces by which computers may be more easily used.

6.2   Cyberspatial Containers

All of the objects discussed above are comprised of information, in the form of binary numbers, which either resides in computer memory or on some other storage medium such as hard disks, floppy disks, optical disks, punch cards, or magnetic tape. Each of these media store programs or other files which may be loaded into RAM. Often, storage media are accessed by computers as part of the flow of a program where there may not be enough room in a computer's RAM for all of the information upon which a particular program acts. Until it reaches an output device, all information in and amongst digital computers, including in various storage media, exists in binary form.

All storage media are a sort of substrate within or upon which the various objects above subsist. As space is to ordinary objects, so storage media are to cyber-objects. There is no commonsense reason to consider any one form of storage medium differently from another. RAM, ROM, optical, and magnetic media all store information in the form of bits. Each is interchangeable with the other in that each may store information. RAM differs from "read-only" media, such as ROM, in that it may be written to and read from. But other read/write media, such as magnetic disks, tapes, or recordable optical disks, may function as does RAM. RAM is more suited to use in computation only because of the speed with which it may be accessed. Otherwise, all read/write media may be used interchangeably. Each serves as a repository for information to be called upon for processing when necessary.

All storage media are themselves commonsense objects. They are all objects which take up space and which may be directly perceived. But storage media are also a substrate for cyber-objects such as those discussed above. In this way, cyber-objects are ontologically dependent upon storage media for their existence. Storage media do not exist in cyberspace, but rather cyberspace may be said to exist in, or by virtue of, storage media. In light of the fact that all storage media themselves have extension, there is no reason to doubt that cyber-objects have extension—they take up space—in their existence in or on the media which themselves take up space. Cyber-objects, composed as they are of bits stored on storage media, have extension just as the words on this page take up space by virtue of the fact that the paper upon which they are printed takes up space.

6.21 Legal Confusion about Storage Media

The law, as discussed in previous chapters, treats machines differently from novels. It is certainly not by virtue of being extended in space that each is treated differently. Clearly, it is the *function* of each that calls for differing treatment. It is thus interesting and problematic that the law treats information (bits) contained in storage media as either a machine or a "written" work (like a novel) or sometimes both. As I discussed above, there is no commonsense or functional difference amongst storage media which may function interchangeably. What then justifies the courts' inconsistent treatment of cyber-objects depending on what storage media they subsist upon?[2] Why would a pre-programmed ROM be patentable while the same program on a disk might be amenable only to copyright?

6.3 Input and Output Devices

Processors (ROM which direct computation and allocate system resources), storage media, and input/output devices comprise the three main elements of modern computers. Information flows amongst these three elements when computers function. Cyberspace could conceivably exist absent input or output devices, but it would be of little use. Input and output devices are necessary to make the results of computation accessible to humans. Input devices include: keyboards, mice, trackballs, scanners, microphones, video cameras, and modems. These devices all take real-world, analog information, which exists in forms which we may directly experience and typically understand, and turn that information into binary form. Output devices include: moni-

---

2. As evidence of this confusion, the Third Circuit Court of Appeals recently stated: "The Internet is not a physical or tangible entity, but rather a giant network which interconnects innumerable smaller groups of linked computer networks." *A.C.L.U. v. Reno*, CV-96-963 (3d Cir, June 11, 1996). What could possible justify this strange statement? Certainly, all of the things which make up the Internet are both physical and tangible.

tors, printers, and plotters. These devices turn binary information into analog form.

6.31   *Philosophical Confusion Regarding Output Devices*

Output devices seem to cause confusion about the nature of cyberspace. The pictures and representations of three-dimensional space which may be conveyed through output devices (for instance, through virtual reality interfaces) are simply pictures, composed of bits and translated into analog images. There is no more space involved in such representations than that which is actually required to display such images. Like paintings at the Louvre, the representations of virtual reality are illusions of space. There is as little point in investigating the metaphysics of virtual reality as there is in seriously investigating the metaphysics of the Mona Lisa. Everything which comprises virtual reality is described above; bits, bytes, words, algorithms, and programs interact in such a way as to display pictures on screens or binocular goggles. Input and output devices act only as means for humans to convey meaning through the medium of cyberspace.

6.4   Networks

A network is a group of computers linked together in such a way as to allow information to move amongst them. The linking takes place via copper wires, fiber optics, or infrared or radio transmission. Bits travel in networks just as they do within and amongst computer chips. 1's and 0's exist in the form of electrical, optical, or radio impulses or charges which travel among computers on a network.

Networks seem to complicate discussions about the nature of cyberspace. This confusion is due to the fact that, as with other aspects of cyberspace, many discussions of networks confuse form with function. In fact, the functionality of a network is like that of a computer, only on a larger scale. Computation may occur over a network just as it may on a single computer. All that is involved in either is the movement of bits among processors, storage and input or output devices.

Networks, specifically the Internet, have come to be synonymous in popular culture with the concept of cyberspace. This is due in part to the origin of the term in the works of William Gibson in which cyberspace is conceived of as a vast, international computer network into which users literally plug their brains and experience a "consensual hallucination" in which information is represented as three-dimensional objects. The Internet is not *quite* like this yet and it may never be. Even if it were, information in such a cyberspace would exist in the form of bits which would be *represented* as three-dimensional objects as in virtual reality.

Networks and the Internet are no more or less elements of cyberspace than any other aspect of computers. Cyber-objects exist in cyberspace as groups of bits in various storage devices. Cables and fiber-optics which connect computers on a network also act as storage devices inasmuch as they contain bits.

6.5 Function and Meaning in Cyberspace

Functionality appears to be the basis for distinctions drawn in the legal categories of intellectual property. That is, machines and processes appear to function differently than do novels, and the law of intellectual property differentiates amongst these types of objects by applying two very different schemes of protection: patent and copyright. The purpose of machines seems even more clearly different than that of novels. Novels serve the purpose of conveying information to others, while machines and processes serve to act upon the world, not necessarily simply to convey information. Yet the law of intellectual property has found, in computer-mediated phenomena, objects which are not so easily distinguished by purpose or function. These objects have consequently been afforded the protections of both copyright and patent. Either computer-mediated phenomena are objects which differ from machines, processes, or novels in some important way, or the distinctions drawn amongst the usual objects of intellectual property law are suspect. The next chapter shall explore these two possibilities.

7

Artifice and Expression

So far, I have set forth the distinctions that are made in the practical and legal world amongst various types of objects belonging to the class of legal objects called Intellectual Property. Now I shall examine the bases for these distinctions and show that they are not founded upon any sound theoretical basis.

7.1 Distinctions amongst Similar Objects

I have discussed at length the fact that the law of intellectual property, which has typically encountered no difficulty in distinguishing amongst machines, processes, and expressions, has somehow fit computer-mediated phenomena into all three of these previously distinct categories. This is a state of affairs with significant practical and theoretical implications. It points either to the fact that computer-mediated phenomena are a special type of object, or that the categories ordinarily adhered to in intellectual property law are somehow faulty. Let us assume first that cyberobjects are a special type of object.

7.11 Special Characteristics of Computer-mediated Phenomena

A program, as discussed in the previous chapter, consists of algorithms and data, encoded in bits which, when introduced to computer hardware (the switches and storage media which comprise computers), cause a computer to produce certain output. For instance, a computer chess game is comprised of numerous algorithms which may produce a picture on a monitor of a chess board. Representations of chess pieces may be moved on the representation of the chess board. The computer will calculate, using algorithms based upon those which chess players ordinarily use, how to move the representations of its chess pieces on the represented chess board. How do these various aspects of a computer chess program exist?

Every aspect of the program itself exists as bits on some form of storage medium. Those bits move amongst the various components of a computer (its processors, storage media, and input/output devices) according to algorithms which are also encoded as bits. All of those bits take up space, in the forms of switches in RAM, charges or etchings on magnetic or optical disks, and as pulses moving through wires or fibers. Why is it so important to remember that bits, like all other media of expression, take up space? The question should be, why is it so easy to forget?

It is a common and regrettable mistake that, when discussing computer-mediated phenomena, people confuse form with function. That is, there are significant properties of bits which make them seem special, namely their ease of transport and reproduction. Information which is digitally encoded is easily conveyed over great distances, and easily copied. Objects in cyberspace are therefore readily distributed and reproduced. Although perfect copies of everyday objects can be made, it is not so easily done. Many duplicate photographs may be made from the same negative, but exact copies in the analog world are difficult to make. Slight variations in exposure, for instance, will inevitably occur and make exact duplicates difficult to produce. Digitized photographs may be duplicated exactly and much more quickly than the analog kind. Moreover, digitized photographs may be transmitted over networks without loss of quality so that the original and the copy which is received are indistinguishable. Although digitized expression and analog expressions are distinct in their form (but of the same substance), they serve the same function—namely, each conveys meaning.

One common mistake is to conflate *information* with *expressions*. Bits are *not* information, they are a medium by which information is conveyed, stored or retrieved. John Perry Barlow repeatedly makes the mistake of confusing information with the media by which information is conveyed. He states blithely:

Once [all expressions are available on the Net], all the goods of the Information Age—all of expressions once contained in books or film strips or records or newsletters—will exist either as pure thought or something very much like thought: voltage conditions darting around the Net at the speed of light, in conditions which one might behold in effect, as glowing pixels or transmitted sounds, but never touch or claim to "own" in the old sense of the word.[1]

Barlow does not explain how information conveyed in the form of bits is even "very much" like "pure thought" just because it is transmitted and reproduced so readily. Nor is the fact that one cannot touch or "own" those bits proof that they are unlike other media of expression.

Moreover, it is simply not accurate that one cannot touch or own bits. I own the hard drive on which this manuscript is encoded in the form of bits. Furthermore, if I own a copyright to the phrase "to err is human; to forgive, divine," whether typeset or encoded as bits, then I have the exclusive right to reproduce, distribute or perform those words for profit. My copyright does not exclude another's *use* by way of utterance, reading or quoting that phrase. I cannot own that phrase in the sense that I own a garden hoe, whether digitally encoded or reproduced upon paper in text, by virtue of differing legal schemes regarding ownership. The only differences between digitally encoded and expressed information, and that which is encoded and expressed in analog form, are differences in degree. It is *easier* to reproduce and transmit digital expressions. This does not mean that digital and analog expressions are different in *kind*.

In fact, there is no good reason to believe that an expression is significantly different when it is stored or transmitted in digital form than when it is stored or conveyed in analog form. The differences in degree cited above do not lead to the conclusion that there are any differences in kind.[2] Unfortunately, it is easy to

---

1. John Perry Barlow, "Selling Wine Without Bottles," in Ludlow, p. 12.
2. Brian Cantwell Smith notes correctly in *On the Origins of Objects* (MIT Press: Cambridge Mass., 1996), that "[c]omputers turn out in the end to be rather like cars: objects of inestimable social and political and economic personal importance, but not the focus of enduring scientific or intellectual inquiry." It turns out that software is also like cars, in this and every other theoretically relevant respect. Smith's work also utilizes a method of ontology similar to that used herein in its interdisciplinary approach.

make the mistake Barlow makes in conflating form and function. To fully understand this mistake we must look again to the purposes of intellectual property law and try to understand what intellectual property is.

7.2 Ideas and Intention

Intellectual property law protects the expression and, to varying degrees, the use of ideas. Intellectual property rights inhere in such things as machines, processes, movies, books, songs, essays, and so forth. Each of these objects is a manifestation of some idea. For instance, *Moby-Dick* is about a sea captain's obsessive hunt for a whale. The phrase, "a sea captain's obsessive hunt for a whale" expresses an idea which *Moby-Dick* also expresses, albeit the latter does so with greater particularity. Intellectual property law protects only physical manifestations of ideas. In other words, Herman Melville owned, by virtue of copyright law, the right to the particular expression of "a sea captain's obsessive hunt for a whale" in the form of the novel *Moby-Dick*. Other people could think about "a sea captain's obsessive hunt for a whale" and even express that thought if they used words or forms of expression sufficiently different from Herman Melville's. The same is true for patents.

A patent protects a manifestation of an idea. If I patent "flubber," an anti-gravity goo which I may invent,[3] I can protect my right to exclusively produce the substance for a limited period of time. I cannot prevent others from having the idea of "an anti-gravity goo" nor of other uses of the chemical formula for flubber short of producing it.[4] My patent in a product does not prevent the dissemination of the ideas behind the product, but only its manifestation as a physical good. Ideas differ from expressions of ideas in the eyes of the law in that no-one may have property rights in ideas, only their expressions or other manifestations.

---

3. *See The Absent-Minded Professor* (Disney, 1961) and *Flubber* (Disney, 1997).

4. In fact, the patent process requires publishing all the inventive matters of a patent. This serves the purpose of making available the knowledge gained in the world by an inventive product while protecting for the inventor certain limited rights in that invention.

7.21 Expressions and Intention

Expressions must be of intended ideas. Behind everything which may be afforded intellectual property protection, there is at least one idea. Before an idea can be expressed, it must be meaningful. A counter-example of this proposition might be a work of abstract art. Certainly, one of the most perplexing questions one could ask about a Jackson Pollock splatter of paint would be "What does it mean?" or "What is it about?" One might spend a lifetime trying to answer such a question and meet with dubious success. However, the relevant similarity between the works of Jackson Pollock and those of other artists is that artists *intend* to produce works of art although they may not intend each and every element of their artistic works.

In a general sense, a Jackson Pollock painting is "about" splattered paint. Its existence is intended. In this way, even the most abstract works of art differ from trees which are not about anything because they are not the products of human intention. In order to be the subject of intellectual property law, an expression must be intended. This is because intention is necessary for meaning and thus ideahood. The link between meaning and ideahood is, I contend, elementary. Something cannot be both meaningless and an idea. In this way, drop-cloths used when painting walls differ from Jackson Pollock paintings in that the paint splatters on a drop cloth were not intentionally placed for the purpose of creating a work of art, but rather are accidentally placed in unintentional patterns as a result of using the drop-cloths to prevent paint from falling on a floor.

7.21.1 Intention, Expression, and Ideas

In the law of intellectual property a significant amount of energy is devoted to the so-called "idea/expression" dichotomy. Above, I concluded that an expression must be *of* an intended idea. More support is needed for this contention and further explanation of the distinction between ideas and expressions is warranted.

While expressions must be of intended ideas, intended ideas need not ever be expressed. The expression of an idea is simply the making known or manifestation of that idea by way of some medium. When an idea is made known, the form of the expression of that idea is protected, under certain circumstances, and to varying degrees, by the law of intellectual property. The idea itself is never afforded legal protection. What accounts for this dichotomy?

Practical necessity certainly serves as one good reason for treating ideas differently from their expression. For instance, a non-expressed idea cannot be proven to have existed prior to its expression. To afford protection to bare ideas, absent some expression, would simply pose an evidentiary quandary for any court of law. Every such intellectual property case would come down to issues of credibility. Moreover, the purpose of intellectual property law is to promote the development and dissemination of ideas. By protecting the expression of ideas, the law of intellectual property promotes the goal of dissemination.

The intention of the producer is what delineates the bounds of an expression. For instance, sharpening a pencil expresses the idea of a sharpened pencil. The sharpened pencil is an expression of an idea, but there are other man-made *consequences* of pencil sharpening which are not expressions. Pencil shavings are a consequence of pencil-sharpening. They are man-made, but they are consequences of the intent to sharpen a pencil. They are not the object of the pencil sharpener's intention, and they are not expressive. Indeed, it would be quite odd if producing pencil shavings was the intent of an act of pencil sharpening, although it would not be impossible. It is important to distinguish between the unintended and the intended consequences of actions in order to determine which products of human activity are expressive, and which are not.

Expressions and ideas seem to exist independently from one another. While being an expression is a sufficient condition for being of an intended idea, ideas can be held and never expressed. The distinction drawn in the law of intellectual property between ideas and expressions has a sound theoretical basis.

7.21.2 OTHER MAN-MADE OBJECTS

All man-made objects, if intentionally produced, are physical manifestations of ideas and are, in fact, expressions of those ideas. A statue of a Greek hero, for instance, is treated both by the law and by ordinary human beings as an expression of the idea of the particular hero portrayed. The first and most obvious distinction which can be drawn amongst various physical objects is that some are naturally occurring and some are man-made. No naturally occurring object can be correctly termed a form of expression. Conversely, all intentionally produced, man-made objects are forms of expression.

The only relevant distinction which may be drawn between physical objects and expressions is that the latter are always intentionally produced, man-made objects while the former may be naturally-occurring. Expressions are extensions of ideas into the physical world. A sentence, whether uttered or written, is an extension of the ideas expressed by that sentence beyond the bearer of those ideas. Any other form of expression that could be made may be similarly characterized. In fact, all man-made, intentionally produced objects are extensions (manifestations) of ideas into the physical world.[5]

There is a distinction appropriately drawn between expressions and artifacts. Artifacts are expressions which have become fixed in a particular medium such that they are preserved. This distinction is recognized in the current copyright scheme and fulfills certain practical concerns. This is a distinction noted by Peter M. Simons and Charles W. Dement who note:

> We should distinguish therefore a *product* of an action from a result of an action. Any action has results, at the very least, the result that the action has been performed. But a product is something which perdures, if only for a short while. A smoke ring, though it last but a second, is an artifact, as are the short-lived particles produced by particle colliders.[6]

All products of intentional action are expressive, although they may not all be artifacts. The law of intellectual property has

---

5. Randall R. Dipert has noted the dependence of artifacts on intention. *See* his *Artifacts, Art Works, and Agency* (Philadelphia: Temple University Press, 1993). He stated recently, for instance: "artifacts are, if you wish, tools that are intentionally marketed as such." Randall Dipert, "Some Issues in the Theory of Artifacts," *The Monist* 78 (2), (1995), 127. I contend that all artifacts are expressions. Not all expressions are artifacts as Dipert and others have defined the term, however.

6. Peter M. Simons and Charles W. Dement, "Aspects of the Mereology of Artifacts," *Formal Ontology,* ed. R. Poli and P. Simons, (Boston: Kluwer, 1996), 255–276. These authors contend that artifacts could be made by non-humans too. This does not imply that birds should be granted intellectual property protection for their nests, however.

restricted protection to expressions which are also certain types of artifacts because of evidentiary difficulties in proving infringement of other expressions.

There is no good theoretical reason to deny intellectual property protection to any man-made, intentionally produced object. In fact, barring certain other exceptions which are built into intellectual property law, any man-made, intentionally produced object including physical objects and other expressions *will* be amenable to some form of intellectual property protection if sufficiently fixed in some medium. What justifies the two very different schemes of intellectual property protection available for man-made, intentionally produced objects?

7.3 Books and Other Machines

How does a book differ from a machine? Although each might properly be described as an expression (an intended idea, extended into the physical world), the primary function or use of each differs.[7] While the substance of books and machines may be the same, and each expresses ideas, the function of a book is to express ideas, while the function of a machine seems to be something quite different; for instance, to pump water. Pumping water is, however, an expression (manifestation) of the idea of pumping water. The function of a literary passage which expresses the idea of pumping water is to convey the idea of pumping water, although a literary passage will never actually pump water. The function of a water pump, on the other hand, is to actually pump water. Both literary works about water pumps and water pumps themselves are expressive, however, of the idea of pumping water.

7.31 The Evolution of Machines

Machines were, at one time, easy to distinguish from other types of expressions. They consisted of parts that moved in conjunction with one another and acted upon the physical world in pre-

---

7. Actually, a book without content is a machine in itself. A novel consists of expression on at least two levels: (1) the idea of a book is expressed, and (2) the ideas of the story in the book are expressed.

dictable ways. In the electronic age it is possible to design machines without visibly moving parts which may yet serve any number of purposes. Unlike books, machines may be capable of acting upon the physical world while books seem to act only upon humans.

The distinction described above has been blurred because technology has advanced such that the degrees and manners with which machines alter the environment have grown more subtle. A computer, for instance, seems to be nothing more than another medium for information storage, like celluloid, paper, magnetic tape, or vinyl. This may well be the source of the confusion in the law over whether copyright law or patent law should be applied to computer-mediated phenomena. This fact makes it questionable that machines and other media differ at all. If one particularly sophisticated machine seems to be nothing more than a means of information storage and retrieval, then what actual difference is there amongst computers and other media?

Failing to recognize that books are themselves a type of machine is due to the mistake of conflating the medium with the message.[8] A book is a machine which serves as a vehicle for information storage and retrieval, acting on the environment by *displaying* information. The novel, the entity which is afforded intellectual property protection, is distinct from the machine in which it is stored. The machine we call a book, and the machine called a computer, differ from each other only in their degrees of complexity. Each is a medium for information storage, retrieval, and transmission. There is no theoretical justification to treat a computer differently from other machines. Nor is there a theoretical justification to treat information stored in a computer differently from information stored in other machines. Books do not differ from machines, and the information stored in machines is not itself a machine.

Expressions of information are the only things which are afforded the protection of intellectual property law. Expressions, which are manifestations of ideas in the physical world, are a certain type of physical object.

---

8. A mistake first made publicly by Marshall McLuhan and glorified now by numerous others.

It has become clear that while intellectual property is a subclass of all other "physical" property, it is not treated like other types of property. This is because of its special purpose as a "bridge" between unprotectable "information" and the rest of the world of physical objects.

7.4 Expressions and Media

Expressions can take many different forms. One piece of information can be expressed through any number of different media. The idea of a unity can be expressed, for example, through uttering the word "one," by drawing the numeral "1," or by other symbolic representations. Symbols which convey information may be verbal, audible, visual, or tactile. The idea of a unity remains, however, the same.

Intellectual property law is developed to serve two purposes: (1) to protect the fruits of intellectual labor, and thus (2) to encourage the development and dissemination of new ideas. These purposes are often at odds with one another because protection of property necessarily involves placing limits upon another's access to or utilization of that property. The law of intellectual property strikes a compromise between these competing goals by allowing for ownership rights only in certain expressions of ideas and for limited periods of time. There are no rights available over the ideas themselves.

All man-made objects, if intentionally produced, are, in some way, expressive. Patent law protects the expression of ideas via machines, but is very limited in the time for which protections are granted. This is because patents can often foreclose the development of a particular idea when that idea can be expressed in a very limited number of ways. Copyright laws are broader in the length of time for which protection may be granted because the ideas expressed by visual, verbal or auditory symbols may be expressed in a virtually unlimited number of ways simply by the rearrangement of symbols. On the other hand, even minor changes in the arrangement of parts of a machine may render it useless and thus incapable of expressing the ideas of that machine.

The differences between patent and copyright protection are differences only of quantity of protection and not in the quality of their objects. All man-made, intentionally produced objects are expressive. Some ideas can be expressed in only a very limited number of ways. The ideas behind many machines are such ideas. Intellectual property protection for machines is severely limited in time because of this fact.

Ultimately, intellectual property is composed of the same stuff as ordinary property. Expressions exist in the world of physical objects. Intellectual property laws limit the ownership rights an individual may assert over his expressions in order to accommodate the goals of protection of rights in those expressions and dissemination of information. In this sense, intellectual property law is actually a sub-class of property law.

7.5 The Computer as an Expressive Medium

It has taken the development of the computer, which is a very flexible and versatile machine, to illustrate the fact that all other machines are simply media for information storage and retrieval. In fact, all man-made objects, if intentionally produced, are media. Before the development of the computer, the limited nature of machines as media made machines and other more versatile media seem to be significantly distinct, thus warranting different forms of intellectual property protection. Because computers are so good at storing, retrieving, and transmitting information, however, those distinctions seem to have blurred. This has caused confusion in the applications of the law of intellectual property to this particular medium. The proposition that all man-made intentional objects are media could lead us to either: a) criticize the entire distinction between machines and other media; or b) determine which practical concerns behind the law of intellectual property warrant what sort of treatment of computer-mediated phenomena. I will consider these possibilities next.

8

A New Ontology
of Cyberspace

The current ontology of cyberspace, as expressed in the law of intellectual property, is inadequate and must be replaced. It is inadequate because it has created a paradox. Patents could not be obtained for expressions and copyrights were not available for utilitarian objects until software was developed. Now, computer-mediated phenomena vie for equal treatment by what were once thought to be two competing categories of being.

The current law must be replaced with one whose ontology is internally consistent. Paradoxes in the law often result in inequity and injustice. A new ontology of intellectual property is needed which will accommodate computer-mediated phenomena and other emerging technologies.

8.1 The Roots of the Current Legal Ontology

The two competing schemes of intellectual property protection owe their development to a distinction which was drawn between those expressions which are considered to be primarily *artistic* or *aesthetic* versus those which are considered to be primarily *utilitarian*. The prohibition in the patent law which prevents patents from being issued for expressive works is really a prohibition against patenting those expressions which do not also primarily serve a utilitarian end. All machines, indeed all man-made objects, if intentionally made, are expressive. But patent law is applied only to expressions which also serve a "useful" purpose. No one can patent a machine which has no use. This simple caveat, which is clearly expressed in the patent law, indicates where the legal ontology has really divided the world. The existing legal ontology distinguishes not among inventions, processes and expression, but between *useful* expressions and *less*-useful expressions. This is why a Rube Goldberg invention cannot be patented, although it might be considered to be art.

8.11   Utilitarian Expressions

The strict time limits applied to the grant of monopolies over expressions which are primarily utilitarian reflect the recognized importance of releasing useful arts into the public domain. The patent system, by requiring patent claims to be published at the same time as strict monopolies over the disclosed art are granted, recognizes that the public good is best served by requiring useful expressions to become publicly available in a short period of time. Human progress requires that utilitarian items eventually be available without the burdens of monopolies and their associated costs. The patent system's grant of a limited monopoly also recognizes that invention is not typically carried out for altruistic reasons, but rather out of the motive for profit. The compromise which is struck in the patent system is a strict—but limited—monopoly in new and useful expressions.

The patent system has worked, by and large, to promote its competing ends. It has broken down, however, in the face of such new inventive technologies as software and genetic engineering. This is in part because the constitutive elements of utilitarian expressions, made of bits or of DNA, are often obscured even after disclosure in the form of patent claims. That is, patent claims for software need not divulge every piece of an algorithm nor explain its functioning in relation to a program, nor can patent claims for new life forms divulge each aspect of that life form. However, developers of new software and new life forms must now be wary of the possibility of infringing upon patents which they cannot know with certainty already exist.

8.11.1   The Problem with Software Patents

An infringement of a patent occurs when someone produces and sells a utilitarian expression for which someone else has already applied for and received a patent. Infringement of a copyright, however, only occurs if someone *copies* another person's artistic expression. Before a patent can be obtained, a patent search must be done. Such searches grow more complex and expensive all of the time because of the growing number of patents granted. A patent search involves looking through other patent claims made for the art for which the current patent is sought. Although much of this process is now becoming computerized, it is still an arduous and costly task to do any patent search. The result of a faulty, incomplete, or inaccurate search may be even more costly litigation after a new invention comes to market.

After capital has been invested and a new invention has been promoted or even sold, the owner of prior art upon which one might have unwittingly infringed nonetheless has an absolute monopoly over that art. Either a court will enjoin further production and sales of the infringing product and possibly impose damages, or it may be possible to work out a licensing agreement with the owner of the prior art. Both alternatives are expensive. In the world of typical, inventive products, very few inventions make it to market, and those that do often make it there only by virtue of well-funded companies. There are very few inventors who move a product from their garage to the shelves of stores on their own.

Software, however, is a product which is not only readily developed in garages and basements, without much capital, but which is also easily distributed despite a lack of capital. By using the Internet as a medium for distribution, it is now entirely possible for software developers to become millionaires from their basements. However, patent searches in the realm of software development are not only prohibitively expensive, but extremely complicated. While patent applications for utilitarian expressions which are tangible (such as a stapler) must be accompanied by drawings of the invention, claims for software patents need not be so accompanied. Rather, the claims which must be submitted need only adhere to the requirements of the Patent Act which state:

> The specification shall contain a written description of the invention, and the manner and process of making and using it, in such full, clear, concise, and exact terms as to enable any person skilled in the art to which it pertains, or with which it is most nearly connected, to make and use the same, and shall

set forth the best mode contemplated by the inventor of carrying out his invention.[1]

Those seeking patents for software will, as a result of this requirement, and absent a requirement to submit the actual code used, specify their claims as broadly as possible to ensure the broadest possible protection. This has already led to a number of suits, brought by large software manufacturers whose technology-transfer departments churn out patent applications deftly and quickly. These suits often target smaller software companies who do not have the resources to do the patent searches, or even apply for patents, for their works of authorship.[2] Consequently, basement software authors must tread lightly and the threat of suits by big, powerful companies is beginning to push smaller developers out of the market. Unlike garage inventors of other products, software has been a medium of invention which has been relatively accessible and whose tools of production are readily available to nearly everyone.

The media of other utilitarian expressions have never been as readily accessible to inventors due to the prohibitively high costs of manufacture and market entry of most utilitarian expressions. Thus, the question of whether patent law's distinction amongst expressions (useful vs. artistic) is correct has never really been an issue. However, cyberspace is a plentiful medium of inventive expression, as well as artistic, and the inherent paradox of the ontology of intellectual property law was never so apparent as it is now. This paradox is not necessarily solved by resort to a distinction between utilitarian and artistic expressions. These categories too are suspect.

8.12 Artistic Expression

Utilitarian expressions are not all treated equally. Only those which are not embodied in language are afforded intellectual property protection. Utilitarian expressions embodied in language

---

1. U.S. Patent Act Sec. 112.
2. For details of this problem, see The League for Programming Freedom "Against Software Patents," in Ludlow, p. 47.

are called "utilitarian works" in the law of copyright and are not copyrightable. Such works include recipes, instructions, and descriptions of processes. Again, the legal scheme has carved out an exception. Specifically excluded from protection is any expression whose public use overrides concerns of awarding individual property rights and concomitant profit rights for authors of certain expressions. Rights inhere in only those portions of utilitarian works which are not purely utilitarian. If, for instance, I compose an original tune to accompany my recipe for cherry pie, then the original tune is amenable to copyright though the recipe itself will not be. This is so despite the fact that a recipe may be written in any number of different ways, with different syntax, words or languages. There is certainly an arbitrary line at which a utilitarian work becomes a non-utilitarian work. What makes the choice of phrase or words in a recipe not artistic?

Despite this exception to copyright, cookbooks are regularly written and sold, not necessarily due only to the recipes which they contain, but certainly due in part to the original forms they take. If recipes are freely copied, as indeed they are, why do authors of cookbooks continue to profit? It is because of the non-utilitarian elements of those cookbooks, or the embellishment of the bare "facts" of the recipes they contain with pictures, celebrities, anecdotes, jokes, and so forth, that people choose one cookbook or other utilitarian work over another. How then do utilitarian works differ from non-utilitarian ones? The following figure illustrates the correct ontology of intellectual property:

FIGURE 8.1

The Commonsense Ontology of Intellectual Property

Man-Made Objects, Intentionally Produced

Primarily Utilitarian ———————— Primarily Aesthetic

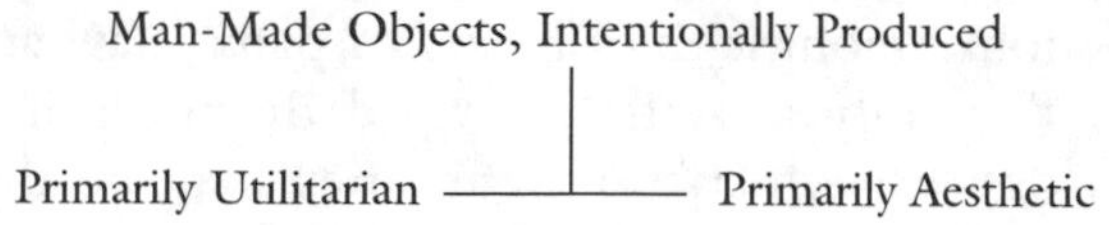

There are certainly no new stories under the sun. Every basic form of story has been told before and since Aristotle described those basic forms.[3] People continue to buy books and see movies

---

3. Aristotle, *De Poetica*.

and plays. As discussed earlier, the basic idea behind Joyce's *Ulysses* is no more amenable to copyright protection than is a recipe. In fact, there are countless unprotectable elements in *Ulysses* and, indeed, in every work of fiction. Nonetheless, whole works of fiction are assembled from unprotectable elements and only a very small number are illegitimately copied for profit.

The distinction between utilitarian and non-utilitarian expression in linguistic media is one that, even were it possible, I could not make. Rather, I contend that the law treats this distinction as a sort of fiction in the understanding that there are no *purely* utilitarian works. Legal action is only necessary to protect those elements of utilitarian works which are sufficiently detached from their non-aesthetic utility to warrant protection as original "artistic" expression.

Copyright law protects only those elements of expressions which are purely aesthetic and original. Anything which has as its primary utility some non-aesthetic purpose is considered to be utilitarian. But how is aesthetic pleasure not a use? If an object's primary purpose is in providing aesthetic pleasure, then its utility is aesthetic. *All* man-made objects intentionally produced serve either a primarily aesthetic or non-aesthetic purpose and each has utility. We are beings which have traditionally placed differing importance on aesthetic versus non-aesthetic utility, and have developed two schemes of intellectual property protection according to this dichotomy of preferences.

8.2 Expressions and Man-Made, Intended Objects

The computer has helped to establish that there are no clear or valid distinctions amongst the objects of patent law and those of copyright. The only potentially valid distinction which has emerged is one for which no clear lines may be drawn—that between aesthetic and other utilitarian objects. The current legal ontology has often drawn its distinctions not upon this basis, but rather upon the basis of the particular media of expression used. The legal ontology has recognized that aesthetic media are many in that copyrightable objects may include written, sculpted, painted, sung, or played works. Patent, on the other hand, has only encompassed expressions in "physical," not linguistic, oral, or auditory media. Every patent which issues must have, as its end, some "tangible" product, or something which may be easily held, touched or which is typically called a "thing." The subjects of patent law protection have been those objects whose utility is closely linked to the particular form of its expression, and whose perceived utility outweighs any injustice which might result from foreclosing expression of that idea by others.

Computers are machines which, whenever they are re-programmed, become another machine. A loom, for instance, could be "hardwired" to produce only one pattern or any number of certain patterns and none other. Loom A, wired (constructed) to produce pattern A, would have certain differences of construction that would make that loom clearly different from Loom B, which is constructed to produce pattern B, and so on. A Jacquard loom is a more versatile loom than A or B in that, by accepting programming, it may produce any number of patterns depending upon the particular program. A particular Jacquard loom becomes a different machine when programmed with program A than when programmed with B. Its product changes as do the particulars of its functioning.

Computers are just extremely complex and versatile Jacquard looms. They are machines whose particular forms and functions vary in relation to the variety of programming they may accommodate. As in languages, whose flexibility accommodate a possibly infinite number of forms of expression for any general idea, computers may be programmed a possibly infinite number of ways. This flexibility has demonstrated that atoms and bits, like language, are just other media of expression. It has only been the degree of flexibility of particular media which has justified distinctions amongst them. However, these distinctions have blurred with the computer. They are certain to blur even more.

Nanotechnology will make every conceivable type of object programmable. Soon, every type of object will be able to be programmed at the atomic level. Nanotechnology involves the use of miniature robots to construct things atom by atom. Like genetic engineering, which involves programming of DNA to create new life-forms, nanotechnology promises to afford humans the ability to construct a possibly infinite variety of new objects. As everyday objects become the subject of programming via nanotechnology, the distinctions which the current law of intellectual property has drawn will further blur. The problems which have emerged in the law of intellectual property regarding computers will be repeated in the law concerning nanotechnology, and are already being faced in disputes regarding genetically engineered life-forms. Are new life-forms, which are created by programming DNA, the subject of copyright or patent? The faulty law of intellectual property has already regarded new life-forms as the subject of patent law, despite the fact that DNA, like computer code, is also a clearly expressive medium. The current ontology must be reworked to accommodate this and emerging technologies which have shown that all media, from machines to DNA to bits, are expressive media. A new ontology of intellectual property is necessary.

8.3   A New Ontology of Cyberspace

The law of intellectual property correctly recognizes that authorship of new expressions must be motivated by profit for innovation to flourish. Copyrights and patents grant authors limited monopolies over the forms of their expressions in order to motivate them and others to develop new expressions. The copyright law grants a monopoly which is narrower in scope but broader in range because the perceived utility of aesthetic innovation is less than that for the subject of patent law, and because the range of forms of possible aesthetic expression is so broad. The greater the perceived utility of an expression, the shorter the time span for which a limited monopoly is granted. The public utility of new expressions is recognized in the law of intellectual property by the fact that those rights which inhere in works of authorship are limited in time, unlike property rights in chattels or lands which may be conveyed *ad infinitum*.

The creation of intellectual property law, which ultimately derives from positive law-making and has no common-law roots, *creates* rights rather than finds them. That is to say, rights to ownership of chattels were recognized to inhere naturally in free men who legitimately came to own those chattels. The common-law right of ownership, from which states derive their right to punish theft, is not a creation of the positive law, but is part of the natural law.[4] Intellectual property rights had to be created because of the natural tendency of ideas, once expressed, to spread and flourish. In order to guarantee profits for the creators of original expression, some means of limiting the spread of new ideas was created. Before the law created intellectual property rights, authors had to protect their creations by secretiveness. Secretiveness works in opposition to the other major purpose of intellectual property law—promoting the dissemination of new ideas.

8.31   Practical Shortcomings of the Current Scheme

Aside from the legal paradox and theoretical quandary which the current legal ontology has created in the classification of software, other practical problems warrant a rethinking of the current scheme. Opponents of intellectual property protection for software often cite the ease with which software can be copied as an argument for removing all protection. Software pirating is commonplace and few people who have computers legitimately own every piece of software in their possession. The computer software industry estimates its losses to piracy in the millions per year.[5] At the same time, the software industry continues to reap huge profits as personal computers become more pervasive in people's homes. Few owners of pirated software are prosecuted, however, because of the practical and legal difficulties of tracking down these "pirates." A practical difficulty is determining the owners of

---

4. Or, more accurately a priori law as described by Adolf Reinach. Adolf Reinach's "The A Priori Theory of Right" was originally published in 1913 in Husserl's *Jahrbuch für Philosophie und phänomenologische Forschung*. Adolf Reinach, both a lawyer and philosopher, undertakes to find the "first cause" of laws. Reinach posits an ontologically independent status for law. That is, laws exist prior to their codification or enactment. In this way, the *a priori* theory of law is similar to natural law theory: "the positive law *finds* the legal concepts which enter into it; *in absolutely no way does it produce them.*" Adolf Reinach, "The Apriori Foundations of the Civil Law" John F. Crosby, Trans.) in *Aletheia*, III (1983) : 4. But this status is unlike that posited by natural law theory in that *a priori* law comes not from a higher law, but rather it is something which is inseparable from people and their relations to each other and to objects. It is just necessarily so, under a certain circumstance, that a claim, right, or obligation exists. Legal concepts and categories, according to Reinach, exist prior to the positive codes which may embody them. More will be said of this in the next chapter.

5. *See* "Pirate Editorial: So You Want to be a Pirate" in Ludlow, p. 109.

illegitimate software; a legal difficulty is executing the searches and seizures necessary to prosecute them. When the majority of computer owners are criminals by virtue of their ownership of illegitimate copies of software, it is not only a practical impossibility to punish all of the wrongdoers, but it would be a public relations nightmare. Software authors also depend on personal computer owners to *buy* their software, which computer owners by-and-large do. Most pirates are also legitimate owners of software. The software manufacturers have thus tread a fine line in encouraging legitimate ownership of software while trying not to alienate software owners whose entire software collections may not be legitimate.

8.31.1 Undue Burdens

The war against pirating is being determined by technology, not public relations. Prosecutions have focused not on the average computer owner who may own a few copies of illegitimate software, but on those who *profit* by the illegal distribution of illegitimate copies. Bootleggers are those who package illegal copies and try to sell them as legitimate copies; anyone who copies a friend's legally obtained copy is a pirate. Bootlegger busts and prosecutions are carried out with high visibility to make the point that the software industry takes bootlegging seriously, and in the hopes of striking fear into the hearts of everyone who may have a pirated version of WordPerfect on their hard-drives. Software has also become bigger and more cumbersome, often requiring tens of floppy disks to back it up, but more often stored on CD-ROM, which have become the medium of choice for software publishers. CD-ROM are difficult for the average computer owner to make illegitimate copies of and often require installation on a user's hard-drive to function properly in tandem with the original disk. Moreover, over the years, software prices have come down as the medium of computers has spread. This has made pirating less attractive, especially in the rare instances (becoming less rare) where user manuals prove necessary and helpful for novice users.

Extending patent protection to software poses a practical problem regarding the prosecution of pirates and bootleggers. As discussed previously, patent infringement actions are expensive and complex. The standards and methods of proof become especially difficult to manage in software patent infringement actions in light of the vagaries inherent in software patent claims. In such cases, the code itself may be put under scrutiny and expert witnesses may be necessary to determine infringement. Copyright claims, on the other hand, are cheaper and easier to prosecute. The varying burdens of these forms of litigation become very important if one considers the possibility of having to prosecute pirates as well as bootleggers.

The remedies available for infringement of intellectual property rights are typically personal remedies, rather than state-sanctioned prosecution. Criminal prosecutions for copyright and patent infringement consume precious funds which the voting public would often rather see used to prosecute violent criminals. Bootleggers do not elicit the sort of fear or anger which murderers and drug peddlers do. It is difficult to justify the expense and complexity of maintaining two very different forms of prosecution for one crime. One scheme of legal protection should suffice.

8.31.2 THE HINDRANCE OF INNOVATION

It is certainly true that copyright litigation has been a real concern for software developers since software was first deemed amenable to copyright. However, the costs and burdens of defending copyright infringement actions are much less than for patent infringement actions. Software start-ups that have to defend against patent actions often end up going out of business or being subsumed by larger companies with coffers which are well-stocked to prosecute such actions. The threat of patent infringement actions and the costs of expensive patent searches which must be made before authoring new algorithms both act to stifle the entrance into the market of new software. In this instance, patent clearly threatens to stifle the introduction of new technologies and the dissemination of new ideas. This runs counter to one of the primary goals of intellectual property law.

8.32 *Alternatives to the Current Scheme*

Because the law of intellectual property is entirely the creation of positive law, one possible (albeit far-fetched) approach to the practical and theoretical problems discussed above is to scrap the

law of intellectual property altogether. It is not terribly difficult to
conceive how a lack of intellectual property protection would
affect innovation and technological progress. One model for how
it might do so may be the early days of software development.
Another model exists in the form of certain highly successful currently existing software companies.

8.32.1 A WORLD WITHOUT INTELLECTUAL PROPERTY

Before intellectual property laws were created, profits made by
innovation were guarded by secrecy. Secrecy was a sufficient protection where the ability of the general public to reverse-engineer
and thus reproduce the products of innovation was lacking.
Agreements entered into among those with the intellectual and
physical means of producing innovative products sufficed to
ensure continued profits for authors of new modes of expression.
As both the intellectual and physical ability of potential actors in
the marketplace climbed, however, simple secrecy was no longer
enough to secure the profits of a monopoly. Laws were created to
ensure the protection of authors and inventors over their works.
But this theory of the evolution of property rights in expressions
depends upon an assumption that innovation is limited and that
profits from innovative expressions will disappear in the absence
of a state-sanctioned monopoly.

Monopolies arise in a marketplace naturally. Large competitors
are often able to push smaller competitors out of the market or
absorb them. But monopolies often fall too as the marketplace
picks some innovative expressions over others according to rules
which none of the players can know. A look at the early days of
software development shows that, even in the absence of intellectual property protection, innovative expression thrived. Before
copyright was clearly extended to software, software was written,
exchanged and used. Even before intellectual property protection
for player-piano rolls became possible, they were made and sold.
Player-piano rolls and other software were in demand by those
who had media with no content. Even after personal computers
began spreading into homes, and even after copyright protection
was statutorily extended to software, personal computer owners
were writing and sharing software. Authors of software shared
their code, delighting in their abilities to simply make their com-

puters do something. This code was distributed freely in computer magazines, with its author's names prominently displayed, and many of the gifted software authors of today began by hacking code for fun and fame. At the same time, software authors learned they could make small profits and pay for their computers by asking for small donations like street performers with open hats.

The ideas of "freeware" and "shareware" developed as means of funding software authors without resort to the expense or formal complications of intellectual property protection. These concepts indicate that people will pay for the value they perceive in an object, even where it is possible for them to duplicate that object themselves. The concept of shareware has not disappeared, rather it has taken off considerably, serving as a means of entry into the marketplace for those software authors who use it effectively.

Recently, the success of the computer game *Doom*, by Id Software, indicates the potential for shareware. *Doom* was originally distributed freely over the Internet as shareware. The shareware version of the game included a limited number of game-play levels and a request that, if the shareware owner liked the game, he or she send the company a small fee and they would receive even more game-play levels. Even though *Doom* players now exchange legally produced and distributed game-play levels of their own invention, using design programs also developed and distributed by Id, the shrink-wrapped version of *Doom* has outsold all other computer games with nearly two million legitimate copies sold.[6] Hundreds of thousands of dollars in payments by shareware owners funded the introduction into the market of the shrink-wrapped version. Id has even made the game-play "engines," which they develop for each of their successively complex games, publicly available, leading to the entry into the market of numerous *Doom* look-and-play-alikes.[7] Yet the founders of Id continue to profit and write new software. This is because consumers now pay for the good name of the company from which they purchase the software as well as the quality of the games they produce. Without the benefit of proprietary game-play engines,

---

6. Mark Laidlaw, "The Egos at Id," *Wired* 4.08 (1996), p. 122.
7. *Ibid.*

Doom's authors continually strive to improve their product. This fact points to another shortcoming of intellectual property protection—it breeds complacency.

Monopolies eventually stifle innovation as long as they artificially inflate profits while protecting innovative techniques. Intellectual property protection is a form of state-sanctioned monopoly. In the absence of intellectual property protection, monopolies will arise and fall naturally in accordance with their abilities to quickly innovate and predict market demands. For example, Id Software avoids complacency by constantly innovating and profiting from the reputation they have for improving their products. Even without their shrink-wrapped software sales, which are protected by copyright, Id's profits would be in the millions of dollars. The success of Id stands in stark contrast to the failure of WordPerfect Corporation, whose product used to sell for hundreds of dollars and illegitimate copies of which existed in abundance. The failure of WordPerfect can also be attributed to their failure to innovate and the demise of their reputation due to software which became clunky and slow even as computers grew faster. WordPerfect has recently been passed from unlucky owner to owner; first to Novell, now to Corel. Meanwhile, Id has refused to sell out to its many courting buyers.

Companies like Id stand to beat large software companies which seek to monopolize the marketplace, despite their lack of insistence on proprietary methods of market dominance, simply by the speed with which they innovate. By consistently and quickly improving their product, and beating others to the market, companies like Id can thrive while monopolies flounder. Only the vagaries of software patent protection serve as a possible roadblock to this sort of success.

One possible future is one in which no intellectual property protection exists, but rather market forces themselves are allowed to guide innovation. Id Software's success is an indication of how such a possible future would look. Authors of innovative expressions could profit in such a world only by quickly moving ever more innovative products to market and trading upon their reputations for producing good products. It is conceivable that the speed of innovation in such a world would increase without a significant reduction in profit motive or profit-making.

8.32.2 A SINGLE INTELLECTUAL PROPERTY REGIME

Another possible (and less radical) future, without the pitfalls of the current paradoxical scheme, is one in which a single form of intellectual property protection exists. Copyright might serve as a model for such a regime, perhaps with stricter limits on the time periods for which protection might be available. Since all man-made, intentionally produced objects are expressions, the law of copyright could encompass every object currently protected pursuant to copyright and patent law. Profits continue to be made on objects which have no intellectual property protection now, namely things like rakes and shovels and other, no longer patented machines. These profits are assured by marketing which concentrates often on *aesthetic* distinctions amongst products. Copyright protection, if limited in time to a shorter term of years, could protect all man-made objects. Innovations might be stimulated by encouraging competitors to improve upon existing, protected products such that their improvements are not "substantially similar" to those protected products. In such a regime, of course, the limitation which prohibits copyright protection for utilitarian works would need to be eliminated.

A consistent scheme of copyright protection for all man-made, innovative objects would accommodate emerging technologies too. As nanotechnology and biotechnology improves, and all matter becomes amenable to programming, the number and degree of innovations will presumably grow. Patent law, with its complexity and cost, will be insufficient and too burdensome to accommodate the explosion of innovation these technologies will bring. A modified copyright scheme would avoid these pitfalls.

Finally, a consistent scheme of intellectual property protection would alleviate the theoretical inconsistencies which exist in the current law of copyright and patent. These inconsistencies are serving as limits to growth and innovation, even as the tools of growth become more powerful and available to more potential players in the market.

9

Implications of the New
Ontology of Cyberspace

At the outset, I mentioned some of the real problems which are beginning to emerge as a result of confusion about the nature of computer-mediated phenomena. In the last chapter, I suggested adopting a revised ontology, in which there would be equal treatment for all computer-mediated phenomena and other man-made objects, if intentionally produced. Such an ontology would avoid the practical and theoretical problems which the current ontology creates. Moreover, the investigation of the ontology of computer-mediated phenomena, through criticism of the existing legal ontology, serves as a model for ontological investigation of any object.

9.1 Cultural Objects

The ontology I have outlined starts from a rejection of metaphilosophical questions as irrelevant. This starting point may already be a point of contention for some. If, for instance, one deems it important to decide whether computer-mediated phenomena are "real" or "abstract" (or ideal perhaps), then the ontological approach which I have attempted to employ will probably be unsatisfying. However, the present ontological approach, through commonsense ontological investigation, helps clarify the practical world while still offering sound theoretical bases for criticism of existing ontologies. By exploring the ways in which various objects are perceived and categorized in existing ontologies, and by criticizing the bases for such categorizations, flaws in existing ontologies may be revealed. In this work, I have pointed out an inconsistency in the legal ontology of computer-mediated phenomena and offered an alternative ontological approach which is internally consistent and practically useful. In so doing, I have worked from the narrow scope of the legal ontology of computer-mediated phenomena to the broader scope of the legal ontology of property in general, and of intellectual property in particular. The broad assumption upon which this approach rests is that there are such things as cultural or social objects.[1]

9.11   *The Origins of Objects*

In preceding chapters I have examined a certain naive ontology (the legal ontology of intellectual property) and criticized certain internal inconsistencies which exist within that ontology. These internal inconsistencies have resulted in practical difficulties. Throughout, this project has rested upon the assumption that anything which may be spoken of is an object. Ontology, after all, concerns the categorization of types of objects. I have made the general claim, essential to the new ontology of cyberspace which I propose, that all man-made objects which are intentionally produced are expressions and should be treated similarly. While all such objects should be treated similarly, I do not contend that all of them are precisely the *same*. In fact, man-made objects which are intentionally produced come in all shapes and sizes. Some such objects, all of which are nonetheless *expressions*, are much more easily located in time and in space than others.

All expressions share one property: they originate from purposeful human action. Not all expressions, however, are "fixed" in any particular medium in the same manner as other expressions may be. The legal ontology has delineated certain distinctions amongst expressions based upon commonly-held agreements regarding the relative "fixity" of various expressions. In this way, cultural objects have been defined, owing their origins to decisions made in the culture-at-large about the importance of certain acts and phenomena. For instance, expressions which are "fixed"

---

1. *See*, for example, Searle 1995.

on paper, in statuary, or on canvas, are afforded the protection of copyright, while those which travel in air or radio waves, are not protected until they come to rest in another medium. While an expression traveling in air waves may be identical in all relevant respects to one recorded on audiotape, certain practical concerns, and possibly cultural biases, impelled the distinction drawn in the law of intellectual property which affords one protection and the other no protection.

9.12   Other Legal Objects

I mentioned earlier that a complete ontology of the law would account for all legal objects including such things as rights and obligations. Rights and obligations owe their origins to both nature and culture as legal objects. It is clear that the various objects of intellectual property are cultural objects. Decisions based upon economics were made which ordered certain types of expressions as protectable and others not so. Certain other decisions guided distinctions which were made amongst expressions which came to be protected by two schemes of intellectual property law. I touched upon the distinction between *a priori* and positive law in the preceding chapter. This distinction is really one amongst two types of legal objects. *A priori* legal objects arise by virtue of necessary relations amongst people and other objects. For instance, the act of promise-making creates a legal object despite the existence of laws or other rules. Intellectual property, on the other hand, exists by virtue of rule-making. Certain rights exist *a priori,* while others are created by cultures. Rights of ownership of chattels, for instance, arise *a priori.* My possession of a particular vase excludes any other person's ownership of the vase by virtue only of the very act of my possession. My rights to possession of objects arise *a priori* too. Claims and obligations also have an *a priori* origin.

9.12.1   A PRIORI LEGAL OBJECTS

Adolf Reinach sought to describe the origin of rights. In doing so, he examined the nature of claims. "A claim arises in the one party and an obligation in the other. What are these curious

entities *(Gebilde)*? They are surely not *nothing*."[2] Reinach explains
that, when claims arise, something in the world changes. A new
object comes into existence. The fulfillment of a claim makes that
claim disappear. This is not due to the enactment of rules or laws,
but is a fact which necessarily arises from the very nature of claims
and acts of promising. These are, according to Reinach, not the
result of "higher law," but are simply "laws of being."[3] He
explains:

> This *a priori* character does not mean anything dark or mystical, it is based
> on the simple facts which we have just mentioned: every state of affairs which
> is in the sense explained general and necessary is in our terminology, *a
> priori*.[4]

The legal object called a "claim" arises through a complex of
both public and private actions. A promise made by person A,
accompanied by both a public (expressed) acceptance by B and an
internal acceptance by B generates a claim.[5] The necessary condition of internal acceptance recognizes that, under certain circumstances, public acceptance alone will not indicate whether a claim
has been generated. Thus, promises made under duress do not
give rise to claims.

Rights also arise through other *a priori* phenomena. The property right in chattels typically arises from the fact of possession.
However, the "right to the possession *(Recht auf den Besitz)*
should of course not be confused with the possession itself . . ."[6]
That is, those things over which I have the right of possession are
said to "belong to" or be "owned by" me, and that belonging is
independent of the fact of possession.[7] Rights of possession arise,
inter alia, through the acts of purchase or trade. What is important is that the *a priori* right of ownership arises *not* through the
enactment of laws or the creation of cultural norms, but through

2. Reinach, 4.
3. *Ibid.*, 135. The distinction made is between natural law theory and *a priori* legal
objects. The former frequently describes just laws as deriving from a deity, the latter does
not.
4. *Ibid.*, 5.
5. *Ibid.*, 2.
6. *Ibid.*, 53–54.
7. *Ibid.*, 54.

various acts and relationships amongst individuals and other objects.

9.12.2 CULTURAL OBJECTS IN THE LAW

A priori rights and other *a priori* objects arise naturally and can exist in a world with as few as two objects. They do not arise arbitrarily. Cultural objects do not share this *a priori* nature. Cultural objects appear by virtue of agreements amongst an arbitrary number of individuals. They do not appear or exist naturally. The distinction drawn in the previous chapter between aesthetic and other expressions was arbitrarily made in Anglo-American culture and adhered to in the law. The categories of intellectual property law are examples of cultural objects. In "Practices of Art," Barry Smith argues that art works are "dependent . . . not only upon the actions of their creators, but also upon *certain correlated activities of an appropriately receptive audience.*"[8] The practice of art is, in the sense that it is determined by certain arbitrary thresholds of actions, neither necessary nor general. Practices in general are social objects. Smith explains: "a given practice depends for its existence upon a group of individuals whose interactions maintain in being the relevant competences."[9] A practice will not arise within any precisely defined or numbered group of individuals, nor will the relevant competences be so precisely definable, although the *manner* in which practices arise may well be described precisely.

All positive laws are cultural or social objects. They arise by agreements amongst arbitrarily defined groups of individuals. Some positive laws reflect *a priori* rights. For example, laws prohibiting theft recognize and arise out of the *a priori* right of ownership. Cultural objects are no more or less real, nor more or less objects by virtue of the fact that they exist by fiat rather than due to necessary relations amongst objects. Positive law often reflects legitimate practical concerns as well as *a priori* objects. The practical concerns which the law of intellectual property has addressed have been the promotion of innovation and the dissemination of

---

8. Nyiri and Smith (1988), 174; emphasis added.
9. *Ibid.*, 183.

new ideas. The question which must be asked is: does the positive law *adequately* address the practical concerns which it was developed to address?

Unlike *a priori* rights, which cannot be justly abrogated by positive law, laws which are not reflective of *a priori* objects may be altered without injustice when they fail to function properly as a means to a particular end. In other words, property rights in chattels cannot be revoked except in derogation of the *a priori* right of ownership. Governmental attempts to revoke property rights in chattels and, to a certain extent, in real estate, are unjust to the extent that such rights exist *a priori,* as do the rights to life and liberty. Intellectual property rights, however, exist only by virtue of cultural agreements and can be altered without derogating *a priori* rights. The alternative approaches to intellectual property law, suggested at the conclusion of the previous chapter, can be implemented without danger of injustice.

9.2 Borders and Cultural Objects

Recently, intellectual property rights have become the subject of an increasing number of international disputes, treaties and agreements. The rise of computer-mediated phenomena as a vehicle for modes of expression has increased the ease of duplication and transmission of expressions beyond national borders. A major concern of authors and distributors of expressions in the U.S. has been the prevalence of unauthorized reproduction and distribution of expressions which may be protected by the intellectual property law of the U.S., but which may not be amenable to such protection abroad. It is not unusual, for instance, nor is it considered unacceptable in most Asian countries for "bootlegged" software and other expressions to be sold on the open market:

> To westerners, copyright is a social bribe, or at least a payoff so as to encourage individual authors to create. In the East, artists gain validity not from creating, but by mimicking previous works. Copying proves the user's comprehension of the core of the civilization itself. To us, copying is plagiarism.[10]

---

10. Alan J. Hartnick, "Intellectual Property Implications of WTO and NAFTA," *New York Law Journal,* 216 (77) (18 October 1996).

The Internet has made the distribution of almost every sort of traditional expression both easy and prolific. Expressions given intellectual property protection in the U.S. have been spread around the world through the Internet, much to the consternation of their U.S. authors. Authors, publishers, and distributors who complain of lost profits due to digital dissemination of their works have lobbied lawmakers to enforce U.S. intellectual property laws abroad. Sparked by the proliferation of unauthorized, digitized distribution of copyrighted materials on the Internet, and the concerns of authors and publishers, the U.S. has recently sought to create and enforce various trade agreements and treaties with many of its trading partners. The thrust of those trade agreements and treaties has been to duplicate the U.S. scheme of intellectual property protection in Asian economies. This attempt has been met with considerable resistance from Asian governments, due in part to the vast market which exists for bootlegged software and other media in those countries where originals are often prohibitively expensive and the boon to these countries' economies which this market has brought. But while authors and publishers in the U.S. complain that their intellectual property rights are being infringed by bootlegging in Asian countries, the rights they are seeking to enforce abroad are culturally generated.

Intellectual property rights do not exist *a priori*. In light of the cultural nature of intellectual property rights, it is not surprising that U.S. efforts to enforce an Anglo-American cultural and legal scheme abroad has met with much resistance. There is simply no similar historical or cultural basis in many countries to recognize those objects created by Anglo-American culture and laws. Either authors and producers may recognize and respect the cultural nature of objects of intellectual property law, or they may choose to try to force the formation of alien cultural objects abroad. It seems likely that the latter course will continue to meet with hostility and contempt while remaining ineffectual in promoting the ends of U.S. authors and publishers. An alternate course would be to abandon the current U.S. scheme of protection altogether and to pursue profits through speedier innovation, better packaging and reasonably-priced quality products.

There is no reason that the model of Id Software (described in detail in the preceding chapter) could not be a model for all production and dissemination of new expressions. Authors make profits not because people fear the legal sanctions afforded by copyright, but because it is easier and cheaper to buy a new book than to copy it. Books are also valued objects in themselves. The packaging of novels, in well-bound books, helps to sell even comparatively expensive hard-cover versions of books that will eventually appear more cheaply in soft-cover. Moreover, there are other cultural pressures, such as desires to be among the first to read a particular book, that contribute to the continued proliferation of "legitimate" copies of books in an age of easy photocopying.

9.3 The Idea/Expression Dichotomy Revisited

One dichotomy which exists in the current legal ontology, and which still holds, is the distinction between ideas and expressions. Ideas can be held and not expressed. The law correctly fails to provide any sort of property right in bare ideas. Rather, the law only provides certain property rights in the expression of ideas. Both patent and copyright law refuse to grant any protection for ideas. However, the law and the courts which interpret the law are confused about where ideas end and expressions begin.

The U.S. Patent and Trademark Office will not grant certain patents where it is believed that what is sought to be patented is an idea. In actuality, no valid patent application could seek to patent an idea because all patents issue only for the *applications* of ideas to products, processes or compositions of matter. Yet, even where such an application of an idea is claimed in a patent application, patents will not issue where an application of an idea to a product, process or composition of matter will completely foreclose the application of that idea to any other. When this is the case, the courts and patent examiners have held that granting a patent would amount to patenting an idea which is expressly prohibited under the Patent Act. Clearly, however, the refusal to grant patents for such expressions of ideas is a practical limitation meant to prevent a complete monopoly over ideas whose range of possible expressions is small. Although courts and lawyers claim otherwise, patents in such instances would *not* amount to patenting ideas.

The new ontology of intellectual property law which I propose recognizes that ideas cannot and should not be protected. The distinction between ideas and expressions is simple: every man-made object which is intentionally produced expresses an idea, but not every idea is expressed. Protecting bare, unexpressed ideas would be both burdensome and unenforceable. I am not interested in pursuing here the nature of ideas. It suffices for the pursuit of a commonsense ontology of intellectual property law to note that an idea may be held and not expressed. Ideas which exist and are not expressed exist at least as thoughts. The purposes of intellectual property law can be met without having to prevent people from thinking about matters in which others might have property interests. Moreover, there are obvious practical and evidentiary problems, as well as privacy concerns, posed by any attempt to enforce property interests in ideas rather than only in their expressions. An expression is that which makes an idea manifest. Ideas which are unexpressed cannot be known to another to be held by the bearer. There is simply no purpose to be served by extending property protection beyond expressions to ideas.

9.4 The Importance of Ontology

Throughout this book, I have stressed the importance of practical considerations in ontological inquiry. Practical considerations and attention to human practices may help to categorize objects, especially where objects are culturally generated. At the same time, ontology itself has practical value. Individuals and cultures create certain objects and, to a certain extent, create naive ontologies. Individuals and cultures categorize objects and thus construct ontologies. However, as is evident from the analysis and argument I have pursued here, not every naive ontology is internally consistent. Inconsistent ontologies, moreover, may eventually result in practical difficulties. This is evident from the problems the law has faced in treating software as both patentable and copyrightable.

The correct practice of ontology can be helpful in avoiding such problems. Objects should at least not be categorized such that one object may fall in two or more mutually-exclusive categories. Because many objects are culturally generated, correct ontology requires not only that the laws of non-contradiction and excluded middle both be upheld, but also that both the bases and purposes of various categories be understood. The categories of legal objects are, in part, cultural. As I discussed in Chapter 3, attempts to create new legal objects which fit into the existing legal ontology will succeed only if the concerns and values expressed by culturally generated legal categories are understood.

Correct ontologies are not only internally consistent, but are consistent with the purposes for which their objects are created. The current ontology of intellectual property is not only internally inconsistent, but is at odds with the purposes which intellectual property law was supposed to serve. The new ontology of intellectual property which I propose, in which all expressions are treated alike, is not only internally consistent, but can serve the purposes of dissemination of new ideas and promotion of innovation which are central to intellectual property law.

9.41 *Legal Ontologies and Legislating*

Over the past hundred years, there have been various efforts to address the problems which inevitably arise due to the Anglo-American systems of common law. The problems, which I have outlined above relating to software and emerging technologies, are accentuated by a legal system in which ambiguities may be simultaneously addressed in contradictory ways by different courts and jurisdictions. The common-law system in the U.S., with its various levels of courts and territorially different standards and jurisdictions, lends itself to anomalous legal ontologies that may take years to rectify through appeals and review. In the early 1900s, various efforts to normalize and standardize the law were made by way of "Restatements" of the law. The Restatement of Torts, for instance, synthesized the conflicting laws of various jurisdictions into a single scheme of tort law. These various Restatements came to be used by lawyers and jurists as authority for legal decisions. Even now, jurists frequently cite Restatements as suggestive authority in support of legal opinions and decisions.

Within the last 30 years, a new trend in a similar vein has appeared. Model codes have been formulated by lawyers and jurists. These model codes make little overt attempt to synthesize existing laws, but instead formulate whole codes of rules and procedures almost from scratch. Often, model codes are adopted by state legislatures, or less frequently by federal legislation, and made into laws. Frequently, the adoption of model codes by state legislatures involves minor changes from state to state made to accommodate local concerns. An example of a widely-adopted model code is the Uniform Commercial Code (UCC) which sets forth the law of contracts and sales in most states. Model codes and Restatements of law are prime examples of attempts at positive rule-making carried out to address the inevitable sloppiness which results from evolving common-law rules.

9.42 Applied Metaphysics, the Common Law, and Technological Change

The recent history of legal ambiguity relating to treatment of computer-mediated phenomena in the law of intellectual property points to difficulties posed by both the common law and positive rule-making. The common law should be best able to deal with the emergence of new technologies and legal objects simply by virtue of the fact that common law is more dynamic than positive law. Changes in the common law can occur as quickly as a legal opinion or decision by a judge. Such changes do not require legislative debate or public assent by vote. It would seem that jurists are best positioned in a common-law scheme to deal with new legal and ontological ambiguities posed by rapid technological change.

On the other hand, positive rule-making, by way of Restatements of law and model codes, is unlikely to be able to deal as quickly with problems posed by rapid technological change. As the speed of technological change increases exponentially, the ability of positive rule-making to keep pace will doubtlessly diminish. Why, though, has the U.S. legal system, which incorporates elements of positive rule-making and common law, been unable to accommodate the legal and ontological challenges posed by rapid technological change of the sort discussed above? One reason is that both positive rule-making and the common law must be guided from the start by correct ontology. The categorization of objects must be done logically and methodically and must be based also upon a correct foundation. Both positive law and common law must also reflect accurately various social and legal goals which often impel the creation or recognition of new objects (cultural objects, for example). Moreover, both the positive law and common law must recognize the existence of certain *a priori* objects. When jurists act in accordance with correct ontology, it is likely that the common law will be better equipped to accommodate legal ambiguities which emerge due to rapid technological change than will positive rule-making. This is an example of the importance of applied metaphysics. Without an acceptance of the methods and values of correct ontology and properly applied metaphysics, legal and ontological mistakes such as those I have described above will continue and multiply.

9.5 Some Answered Questions

Cyberspace is nothing really strange or special. Bits are just another medium of expression. Bits happen to be very malleable and computerized media are particularly flexible compared with other media. Expressions in cyberspace are just as real, and exist in space in the same way as expressions in other media. The term 'cyberspace' is misleading to the extent that it connotes a dimension apart from that of ordinary experience. Electrical charges take up ordinary space as atoms take up ordinary space. The message remains the same despite the medium used for its conveyance. All objects in cyberspace are expressive objects, just as all man-made objects, if intentionally produced, are expressions. All expressions exist in ordinary space and are objects or ordinary experience. Some expressions are easier to locate in space and certain cultural values have impelled distinctions amongst expressions on this basis.

A correct ontology will recognize the importance of those cultural values while also recognizing that all man-made, intentionally produced objects are expressions. This recognition must result in abandoning the false dichotomy between the subjects of patent law and those of copyright.

I have referred at length to Menger and Reinach who are, I believe, important and revolutionary theorists in the field of social objects. My argumentation, however, is not dependent solely on their methods. I do begin with an assumption that there are such things as social or cultural objects and specifically *legal* objects. The bulk of my method is that of commonsense ontology as discussed in Chapter 2. Even without reference to Menger or Reinach, the following points hold:

1. Cyberspace is physical as all its components are physical.

2. The existing ontology of cyberspace, which fits an object into two mutually exclusive categories, is incorrect.

3. All man-made, intentionally produced objects are expressive objects (either primarily aesthetic or primarily utilitarian) and could be treated best by a unified intellectual property scheme.

9.6   Examples and Case Studies

What or where is cyberspace? Is cyberspace a place? Is it a thing? Do cyberspatial entities exist? How do they exist? These ontological questions have never been seriously addressed heretofore. A result of the absence of satisfactory inquiries into these questions has been a confused legal categorization of cyberspace and its objects. Another result has been a general social failure to deal rationally with these objects.

The arguments above have shown that the legal categories which have been applied to cyberspace and its objects have been inadequate. But the law is at least half right. The original instinct that cyberspatial entities are amenable to intellectual property protection is founded upon a proper judgment. Computers are an expressive medium. But then, so is every man-made object which is intentionally produced. The law has perpetuated a confused ontology which categorizes certain artifacts as expressive and others as non-expressive. As shown above, this dichotomy is false. All artifacts are expressions. Cyberspace is a medium composed of silicon chips, copper wires, magnetic tapes and disks, fiber optic cables, and every other component of computers, storage media and networks which stores, transmits and manipulates bits. Cyberspatial entities are the expressions which subsist in the medium of cyberspace. This subsistence is exactly analogous to the subsistence of any other expression in any other medium. Software exists in cyberspace as text exists on paper, or as a statue exists in stone. The expression is distinct from its medium, but wholly dependent upon it as well. What is true for software is also true for data sets, e-mail, web pages, and any other cyberspatial entity.

Example A: Software

A computer program may exist in many forms and on many types of media. The word processor I am using was purchased on CD-ROM and installed onto my hard drive. It consists of algorithms and data sets whose most basic parts are bits. When my computer is off, those algorithms and data sets reside on the hard drive alone, taking up actual space as magnetic charges. One could measure the area which stores the word processing program on my hard drive. This program's spatial and temporal existence is exactly analogous to the existence of these words on this page.

When I turn the computer on and start my word processing program, depending upon the amount of RAM available, all or parts of the program are loaded into the computer's memory in order to "run" the program. But as I discussed above, RAM is as much a storage medium as are disk drives and other such media. In fact, an idealized Turing machine techinically does not distinguish amongst storage media.[11] Has the program changed then when introduced to the computer's RAM from the storage medium? There is no reason to suspect that it has in any theoretically relevant manner. It is, in all respects, the same program as when it resided solely on my hard drive. Its structure and composition remain the same. It remains the same expression in just another medium.

Example B: A Web Page on the Internet

Web pages are just another form of software. Again, they consist of data in the form of bits which reside in some storage medium. Just as with my word processor, my web page resides in a specific

---

11. *See*, A.M. Turing, "On Computable Numbers with an Application to the *Entscheidungsproblem*" *P.Lond. Math.* Soc. 42(2) (1936) : 230–263. A Turing machine consists simply of "an infinitely long, segmented tape and a device that can perform four operations on such a tape, namely: make a mark, erase a mark, move one segment forward, and move one segment backward." James H. Fetzer, "Thinking and Computing: Computers as Special Kinds of Signs," *Minds and Machines,* 7 (3) (1997).

place and occupies a certain space on a hard drvie in Amherst, New York. When you "point" your browser to http://wings.buffalo.edu/~koepsell, you are sending a message across the Internet which instructs my web page's host computer (a Unix machine at the University of Buffalo) to send a copy of the contents of my personal directory, specifically a HTML file called "index.html," to your computer. That file is copied into your computer's memory and "viewed" by your browser. The version you view disappears from your computer's memory when you no longer view it, or if cached, when your cache is cleaned. You may also choose to save my web page to your hard drive in which case you will have a copy of my index.html file. My index.html file remains, throughout the browsing and afterward, intact and fixed.

Example C: A Chat Room

One of the uses of the Internet which provokes some of the more problematic misperceptions of cyberspace is the Internet Relay Chat, or IRC. This utility, and other similar utilities supported by some of the major Internet providers, allows users to connect with each other in real-time "chat sessions," as opposed to simply sending e-mail back and forth. These sessions involve the transmitting of blocks of text across the Internet from one particular user to another, in a manner which is analogous to the transmission of e-mail. These sessions are confined to "rooms," or more appropriately, channels. Where then are users engaged in a chat session? Do they inhabit these rooms? Simply put: no. Chat rooms are analagous to telephonic connections, or conference calls when more than one person is connected. Again, it is the medium which at first appears different, but which in practical, and theoretical effect, is a medium like any other. A chat room is no more a "room" than is a telephonic switch which relays our phone conversations.

9.7 Future Objects, Special Cases, and Unanswered Questions

Even the most carefully considered ontology may not anticipate every possible future object. Although I have tried to anticipate the application of my proposed commonsense ontology of intellectual property to as many potential objects as possible, there is at least one future object which may not easily fit into this ontology. I have argued that all man-made objects which are intentionally produced are expressions and should be treated equally as intellectual property. This proposition is complicated by the possibility of future expressions' abilities to create expressions.

The question of how artificial intelligences should be treated is not fully answered in this ontology. It will be true that artificial intelligences, whether developed in computerized media, genetically engineered, or developed by nanotechnology, will all be man-made and products of human intention. There may be ethical considerations, however, which impel distinct treatment for artificial intelligences as a unique form of expression. Such expressions may have the unique capability of creating expressions themselves. There may be important cultural reasons to distinguish amongst *expressing* objects and other types of objects. A future ontological and ethical consideration will be whether all expressing objects are bearers of certain rights. Whether such objects may be able to form and hold intentions will be a matter of future debate. It is beyond the scope of this work to resolve the problems of artificial intelligences, but it is worth noting that this issue is still open in the face of my proposed commonsense ontology of intellectual property.

Finally, the classification of all man-made, intentionally produced objects as 'expressions' poses some interesting questions regarding the scope of First Amendment protection. Again, this particular question is one for a future work. But it is worth noting that the First Amendment protects not just speech but expression generally. If machines are expressive objects, just as statues are, then to what extent is one's ability to construct a nuclear device, for instance, protected by the Constitution? This and other related questions are vitally important and will be addressed in future works.

9.8 Dispelling the Myths of Cyberspace

The Internet, computer-mediated phenomena, and cyberspace continue to perplex people. They have proven to be versatile tools around which a strong new economy is growing. They permeate our lives professionally, academically, and personally. New communities have formed around these new tools. Businesses have altered ways they operate, and schools have changed the way they educate due to computer-mediated phenomena. It is impossible to envision a future without increased computerization in every level of society. At the same time, the speed with which computer-mediated phenomena are evolving seems to increase exponentially. It is sometimes hard to keep up with the computer-mediated revolution. The spread of the various myths associated with computer-mediated phenomena, those which I have tried to dispel in this work, is in part due to the speed and extent with which the medium continues to change our lives. Quick, expansive changes in the ways in which people interact with each other and their machines may seem almost mystical or other-worldly. It is tempting to think that virtual realities will offer new, thrilling experiences when the world of ordinary experience offers only shrinking frontiers.

Moreover, computers are increasingly less transparent to those who want to try to "look under the hood." Like the world of particle physics, the functioning of computers becomes more and more a matter of faith or belief about the actions of invisible currents on invisible switches. When technologies become impenetrable to ordinary perception, people develop naive belief-systems about their functioning. These belief-systems do not necessarily represent the actual functioning of those technologies.

Finally, computer-mediated phenomena have entered the mainstream only recently in relation to their development. Within the last ten years, tools which were once accessible only to hobbyists, university students and scientists, have become accessible to almost everyone. The popular culture which currently surrounds the Net has much to do with the perceived threat which "the masses" (newbies) pose to the homesteaders of the electronic frontier. Elaborate codes of etiquette, rituals of interactions, and complex lingoes have developed around computer-mediated phenomena as both a means of excluding the late-comers to these media and establishing who really belongs there.

The popular culture surrounding computer-mediated phenomena is full of those who seek to perpetuate myths regarding their nature as belonging to some sort of mystical, special realm. These myths serve the purpose of keeping newcomers indebted to long-time users who must initiate them to this realm. Moreover, these myths support arguments aimed at keeping the Net and computer-mediated phenomena mysterious to law-makers who must then depend upon how they are informed about these phenomena by the gurus when it is time to make laws. Thus, laws like the Communications Decency Act (CDA)[12] recently overturned as unconstitutional by the Third Circuit Court of Appeals and the U.S. Supreme Court, should not be surprising in light of the myths which surround computer-mediated phenomena. The CDA sought to create whole new standards of conduct on the Net which never would be enforceable in any other medium. The drafters of the CDA sought to prevent the dissemination of "indecent" materials on the Internet. The dissemination of "indecent" materials in any other medium is clearly protected by the First Amendment of the U.S. Constitution. The mystique of the Internet, propagated in part by its foremost proponents, helped to convince the drafters of the CDA that the Net was a medium unlike any other.

William Gibson, who coined the term "cyberspace," has recently distanced himself from some of the more worrisome implications of the term. The word connotes a new realm, a place apart from the world of ordinary experience. Recently, Gibson described the root of misperceptions about computer-mediated phenomena:

> It's not [a question of the line] between real and unreal—it's between real and real. The only reason we see that dichotomy [between real and virtual] is because we are old.[13]

Computer-mediated phenomena are expressive objects just like any others. When they are finally treated that way, and the myths which surround them are dispelled, this medium will prove to be the most powerful force for economic and social growth of the Twentieth Century and beyond. Until then, misguided lawmaking and misperceptions in the popular culture about the nature of computer-mediated phenomena will continue to hinder this medium's true potential and stifle its growth.

---

12. Title V of the Telecommunications Act of 1996 (2/2/96) Pub. L. No. 104 Sec. 502, 110 Stat. 56, 133–35; 47 U.S.C. Secs. 223(a) and 223(d).

13. *Wall Street Journal* (26 September 1996), p. B6.

References

Alter, Max. 1990. *Carl Menger and the Origins of Austrian Economics.* Boulder: Westview.

American Jurisprudence. 18 American Jurisprudence [Second], 1974, Copyright Sec. 51.

———. 18 American Jurisprudence [Second], 1974, Copyright Sec. 52.

———. 60 American Jurisprudence [Second], 1974, Patents Sec. 65.

Anonymous. Pirate Editorial: So You Want to be a Pirate. In Ludlow 1996.

Ayer, A.J. 1952. The Elimination of Metaphysics. In *Language, Truth, and Logic.* New York: Dover.

———. *Metaphysics and Common Sense.* Boston: Jones and Bartlett.

Berkeley, George. 1979. *Three Dialogues between Hylas and Philonous.* Indiana: Hackett.

Burk, Dan L. 1993. Patents in Cyberspace: Territoriality and Infringement on Global Computer Networks. *Tulane Law Review,* Vol. 68 (November).

Cantwell-Smith, Brian. 1996. *On the Origins of Objects.* Cambridge, Massachusetts: MIT Press.

Casati, Roberto, and Achille C. Varzi. 1994. *Holes and Other Superficialities.* Cambridge, Massachusetts: MIT Press.

Diamond, Sidney A. 1975. The Historical Development of Trademarks. *The Trademark Reporter,* Vol. 65, p. 265.

Dipert, Randall R. 1993. *Artifacts, Art Works, and Agency.* Philadelphia: Temple University Press.

———. 1995. Some Issues in the Theory of Artifacts. *The Monist,* Vol. 78, No. 2 (April 1995), p. 127.

Disney (movie). 1961. *The Absent-Minded Professor.*

Hartmann, Nicolai. 1953. *New Ways of Ontology.* Chicago: Henry Regnery.

Hartnick, Alan J. 1996. Intellectual Property Implications of WTO and NAFTA. *New York Law Journal,* Vol. 216, No. 77 (18th October).

Heim, Michael. 1993. *The Metaphysics of Virtual Reality.* New York: Oxford University Press.

Ingarden, Roman. 1964. *Time and Modes of Being.* Trans. Helen Michejda, Springfield: Charles C. Thomas.

Johansson, Ingvar. 1989. *Ontological Investigations: An Inquiry into the Categories of Nature, Man, and Society.* New York: Routledge.

Kfia, Lilianne Rivka. 1993. The Ontological Status of Mathematical Entities: The Necessity for Modern Physics of an Evaluation of Mathematical Systems. *Review of Metaphysics,* 47 (1993), pp. 19–42.

Laidlaw, Mark. 1996. The Egos at Id. *Wired,* 4.08, p. 122.

The League for Programming Freedom. 1996. Against Software Patents. In Ludlow 1996, p. 59.

Lessig, Lawrence. 1999. *Code and Other Laws of Cyberspace*. New York: Basic
    Books.
Levy, Steven. 1984. *Hackers: Heroes of the Computer Revolution*. Garden City,
    N.Y.: Anchor Press/Doubleday.
———. 1996. Crypto Rebels. In Ludlow, p. 185.
Ludlow, Peter, ed. 1996. *High Noon on the Electronic Frontier: Conceptual Issues
    in Cyberspace*. Cambridge, Massachusetts: MIT Press.
Mantle, Ray A. 1984. Trade Secret and Copyright Protection of Computer
    Software. *Computer Law Journal*, 4, p. 669.
Menger, Carl. [1871]. *Investigations into the Method of the Social Sciences with
    Special Reference to Economics*. Trans. Francis Nock. New York: New York
    University Press.
———. 1963. *Problems of Economics and Sociology*. Trans. Francis J. Nock. Ed.
    Louis Schneider. Urbana: University of Illinois Press.
Nyiri, J.C., and Barry Smith, eds. 1988, *Practical Knowledge: Outlines of a
    Theory of Traditions and Skills*. New York: Croom Helm.
Pesce, Mark. 1993. The Final Amputation: Pathogenic Ontology of Cyberspace.
    Third Annual Conference on Cyberspace.
Plato. 1954 *Meno*. Trans. B. Jowett. New York: Tudor.
Popper, Karl. 1961. *The Poverty of Historicism*. Second edition. London:
    Routledge.
Quine, W.V. 1951. Two Dogmas of Empiricism. *Philosophical Review*, 60, pp.
    20–43.
———. 1947. On Universals. *Journal of Symbolic Logic*, 12, pp. 74–84.
Reinach, Adolf. 1913. The Apriori Foundations of the Civil Law. Trans. John F.
    Crosby. *Aletheia*, Vol III (1983).
Smith, Barry. 1986. Austrian Economics and Austrian Philosophy. In Wolfgang
    Grassl and Barry Smith, eds. *Austrian Economics*. London: Croom Helm.
———. 1994. *Austrian Philosophy*. Chicago: Open Court.
———. 1995. Formal Ontology, Common Sense, and Cognitive Science. *Inter-
    national Journal of Human-Computer Studies*, Vol. 43, pp. 641–667.
———. 1995. On Drawing Lines on a Map. In Andrew U. Frank and Werner
    Kuhn, eds. *Spatial Information Theory: A Theoretical Basis for GIS*. New
    York: Springer.
———. 1997. On Substances, Accidents, and Universals: In Defence of a
    Consituent Ontology. *Philosophical Papers* (forthcoming).
Smith, Barry, and Leonardo Zaibert. 1996. Law, Ecology, Land, and Credit: An
    Investigation in the Comparative Ontology of Real Estate and Landed
    Property. Research Proposal, http://wings.buffalo.edu/philosophy/
    smith/articles/lz.html.
Simons, Peter M. and Charles W. Dement. 1996. Aspects of the Mereology of
    Artifacts. In R. Poli and P. Simons, eds. *Formal Ontology*. Boston: Kluwer,
    pp. 255–276.
Takatura, Ando. 1963. *Metaphysics: A Critical Survey of its Meaning*. The
    Hague: Martinus Nijhoff.
Von Nostrand's Scientific Encyclopedia. 1976 (Fifth Edition).
Wall Street Journal. Court to Ponder Copyright Laws for Software. *Wall Street*

Journal (28th September, 1995), p. B1.
Williams, C.J.F. 1981. *What is Existence?* Oxford: Clarendon.
Zimmerman, Philip R. 1996. How PGP Works/Why Do You Need PGP? In Ludlow 1996, p. 179.

Statutes

15 United States Code, Secs. 1052 (a)–(d), (f)
17 United States Code Sec. 101.
17 United States Code, Sec. 117
17 United States Code, Sec. 102(a).
17 United States Code Sec. 102(a).
17 United States Code Sec. 109(b).
35 United States Code Sec. 101
The Statute of Monoplies: Statute 21, James I. Chapter 3
Title V of the Telecommunications Act of 1996 (2/2/96) Pub.L. No. 104–104 Sec. 502, 110 Stat. 56, 133–35, 47 U.S.C. Secs. 223(a) and 223(d).
U.S. Copyright Act Sec. 114.
U.S. Patent Act, Sec. 101.

Cases

Abercrombe & Fitch Co. v. Hunting World, Inc, 537 Federal Reporter 2d ["F.2d"] 4 (1976).
Apple Computer, Inc. v. Franklin Computer Corp., 714 F.2d 1240 (3d Cir) *cert. dismissed* 104 S.Ct. 690 (1983).
A.C.L.U. v. Reno, CV-96-963 (3d Cir., June 11, 1996).
Amsterdam v. Triangle Publications, Inc., 189 F.2d 104 (1951).
Application of Freeman, 73 F.2d 1237, 1244 (1978).
Arrythmia Research Technology v. Corazonix Corp., 958 F.2d 1053 (Fed. Cir. 1992).
Baker v. Selden, 101 U.S. (11 Otto) 99 (1879).
CGA Corp. v. Raymond Chance, 217 U.S. Patent Quarterly, 718 (N.D. Cal. 1982).
Continental Casualty Co. v. Beardsly, 253 F.2d 702 (1958).
Diamond v. Diehr, 450 U.S. 175 (1981).
Diamond v. Chakrabarty, 447 U.S. 303 (1980).
Folsom v. Marsh, (C.C.D. Mass. 1941) (No. 4901) Story, J.
Goldstein v. California, 412 U.S. 546 (1973).
Gottschalk v. Benson, 409 U.S. 63 (1972).
Parker v. Flook, 437 U.S. 584 (1978).
Inwood Laboratories, Inc. v. Ives Laboratories, Inc., 456 U.S. 844 (1982).

Johnson Controls, Inc. v. Phoenix Control Systems, Inc., 886 F2d 1173 (9th Cir. 1989).

Mazur v. Stein, 347 U.S. 201 (1954).

Plains Cotton Coop. Ass'n v. Goodpasture Computer Serv., Inc., 807 F.2d 1256 (5th Cir. 1987).

Schering Corp. v. Gilbert, 153 F.2d 428 (1946).

Schroeder v. William Morrow & Co., 566 F.2d 3 (1977).

Step-Saver Data Systems, Inc. v. Wyse Technology, 939 F2d 91, 96 (3d Cir. 1991).

Stern Electronics v. Kaufman, 669 F.2d 852 (2d Cir. 1982).

The Clothworkers of Ipswitch, Godbolt, 252 (Decided at Easter Term, 12 James I) (1614).

Twentieth Century-Fox Film Corp. v. MCA, Inc., 715 F.2d 1327, 1329 (9th Cir. 1983).

United States v. Stefans, 100 U.S. Reporter 82 (1879).

Vault Corporation v. Quaid Software Limited, 847 F.2d 255 (5th Cir. 1988).

Whelan Associates, Inc. v. Jaslow Dental Laboratory, 797 F2d 1222 (3d Cir. 1986) *cert.denied* 107 S.Ct. 877 (1987).

White-Smith Music Publishing Co. v. Apollo Co., 209 U.S. 1, 28 S.Ct. 319 (1908).

Williams Electronics, Inc. v. Arctic International, Inc., 685 F2d 870 (3d Cir. 1982).

Index

Computer networks. *See* Networks
Computer Software Copyright Act, 69
Computer Software Rental Amendments Act 1990, 3n
Continental Casualty Co. v. Beardsly, 53
Contracts, 38, 51–52
Copyright: in computer programs, 51; development of law, 46, 88; direct perception test, 51n, 61; expressions, 53–54, 56–57, 102; historical background, 50, 51, 54, 57, 94; legal ontology of, 59; ordinary observer test, 66; parody, as exception to, 57; performances, 57; protection of software, 4, 17, 65–68, 69, 70, 107, 111; recipes not protected, 100–01; right to reproduction, 56–57, 99; scope of, 49–51
Copyright Act, 59, 67, 68, 69, 70; amendments to, 51, 54, 59, 61, 68, 70
Crosby, John F., 34n
Cultural objects, 117
Customs, 64
Cyberpunk fiction, 11
Cyberspace, 1–3, 11–13, 22, 78–83, 124–25; and copyright, 57n; "Erotic Ontology of," 13, 22; myths about, 1–2, 130; physical nature of, 124–25. *See also* Computer-mediated phenomena
Cyberspatial containers (storage media), 80–81

Data, 59, 85
Data Processing Glossary, 59
Dement, Charles, 91
Diamond v. Chakrabarty, 55n
Diamond v. Diehr, 64
Diamond, Sidney A., 45
Difference Engine, 12n
Digital and analog expressions, 85–88

Digital communication, 12
Digitized photographs, 86
Dipert, Randall R., 91n
DNA, 98, 103–04
Doom, 109

Electronic Frontier Foundation, 6
Electronic switching, 12
E-mail, 5, 6–8, 12, 126–27
ENIAC, 3n
Enigma machine, 6
Epistemology, 23
Expressions: artistic, 89, 97–99, 100–02; as extensions of ideas, 91; fixed in tangible media, 50–51, 114–15, 124; and ideas, dichotomy of, 16, 53–54, 67, 69–71, 73–75, 89–90, 120–21; as intellectual property, 1, 3, 4, 6, 9, 16, 17, 46–47, 56–58, 60, 90, 97–98, 108, 118–19; levels of, in software, 66–68; and machines, 3; media, 89–94; utilitarian, 97–104. *See also* Objects

Fetzer, James H., 126n
Formulas, 63–65, 74
Frank, Andrew U., 15n
Freeware, 109
Freiburger, Paul, 62n
Functionality, 83

Gates, Bill, 62
Grassl, Wolfgang, 36n
Gibson, William, 11, 83, 130
Goldstein v. California, 54
Gottschalk v. Benson, 62
Gopher server, 7, 8

Hackers, 62
Hackers, 61n
Hardware, 59